I0051536

SUPPLY MANAGEMENT STRATEGIES:

3rd Edition

CERM Academy Series on Enterprise Risk Management

Greg Hutchins PE
Quality + Engineering
QualityPlusEngineering.com
800.COMPETE

TABLE OF CONTENTS

Chapter	Page

CHAPTER 1:
INTRODUCTION

The title of the first purchasing book I wrote twenty years ago was: **Purchasing Strategies for Total Quality**. **Supply Management Strategies for Improved Performance** is the title of the second edition we wrote 12 years ago. The second edition described purchasing and sourcing priorities. In this edition, we simplify the title to Supply Management Strategies 3rd Edition. Many things have happened in the last twelve years. We expanded beyond quality. Purchasing has matured. There is more emphasis on business performance improvement and enhancing the bottom line.

WHAT DO WE COVER IN THIS BOOK?

As the title **Supply Management Strategies** implies, we cover the state of supply management, present best practices, and provide guidelines on how to jumpstart your supply chain initiative.

In **Supply Management Strategies**, we explain how to:

- Integrate the disparate elements of supply chain management into a competitive business system.

- Align supply management systems with strategic initiatives and goals.

- Select and develop suppliers according to risk, cost, quality, flexibility, system responsiveness, and overall performance criteria that go beyond traditional cost-per-unit considerations.

- Certify suppliers and partners to establish a common supply management language for communication.

- Use technology to improve supplier partnerships.

- Refine and enhance the manufacturing processes in the supply chain to ensure critical partners focus on core processes and core strengths.

- Foster better communication between partner organizations by using electronic communication tools and methods.

- Emphasize the mutual benefits of supply chain partnering.

- Move beyond a price-focused relationship to a value added re- lationship

- Prepare supply chain executives and managers for their new emerging roles, responsibilities, and authorities

Also, supply chain management hype seems to be drowning out the reality of purchasing. In this book, we separate hype from fiction, focusing on what strategies work.

INTEGRATES MANY FUNCTIONS, TOOLS AND TECHNIQUES

Supply chain management is comprised of many tools and techniques, such as lean, just in time, six sigma, etc. Each of these cutting edge philosophies has a different functional home. Quality or an operating department owns Six Sigma. Materials management owns inventory control. Marketing owns demand forecasting. Manufacturing owns production control and lean production. Engineering owns robust and lean design. Purchasing owns supplier relationships. And, so it goes.

Is there one central coordinating and communicating function for supply issues? No. Does there need to be a group that owns supply chain management if organizations are going to coordinate and resolve supply chain issues? Yes. Where should it reside? The logical owner is supply management or what today is called purchasing.

WHY EMPHASIZE SUPPLY CHAIN MANAGEMENT?

The idea of supply chain management has been around for about 10 years. It's only in the last 5 years, that it has become more popular. We are still at the early stage of supply chain management adoption and deployment in many organizations. In this book we answer basic questions like: "Where do we start?" and "Who knows what is really going on here?"

In terms of total dollar amount, external suppliers provide a significant portion of a manufacturer's product. For U.S. companies, 50% or more of the final price of a product can be the cost of purchased goods. In Japan, it can be even higher. For these reasons, supply chain management is critical to a company's competitiveness.

SUPPLY CHAIN MANAGEMENT SHIFTS

The shift in perceived supplier importance results from trends that will impact most companies over the next several years. These trends include:

- Focus on core competencies and technologies is coupled with the outsourcing of non-core activities.

- All companies feel pressure to innovate and improve continuously in critical performance areas, including build to order, process capability, product quality, product delivery, cycle time reduction, and service improvement.

- Ongoing emphasis is to provide supply system solutions not only provide products.

- Intense worldwide competition pressures all companies to reduce overall supply chain costs.

- Strong leadership commitment, supplier involvement, quality at the source, and continuous improvement throughout the chain are critical success factors.

- Standardization throughout the value chain ensures consistency, such as simultaneous design, lean manufacturing processes, mistake proofing, total productive maintenance, and collaborative teams.

- Streamlined and uninterrupted flow of material through the process chain must be supported by cell manufacturing, 3D printing, blockchain, pull production techniques, flexible operations, rapid machine/process changeover, and customer-supply development.

- Continuous elimination of waste and redundancy is a priority across the value chain.

- Supply chain information requirements must be understood and exchanged with supply-partners.

THE SUPPLY MANAGEMENT READER

This book's audience is supply management professionals. Supply management professionals are not only buyers and supply managers, but involve everyone in the supply value chain, including:

- Product development engineers.

- Manufacturing and production managers.

- Production planners.

- Quality engineers.

- Marketing professionals.

- Distribution professionals.

- Inventory managers.

- Production control managers.

- Logistics professionals.

- Consultants.

- Students.

SCM AS CHANGE, RISK, AND PROJECT MANAGEMENT

We will examine SCM from a number of perspectives, including change management, risk management, and project management. For example, project management is sometimes defined as change management, specifically the ability to manage change or variance from specifications, requirements, contracts, etc. Any movement away from a specification or contract target involves a risk. How these are monitored, controlled, managed, corrected, and prevented from recurring are the fundamental elements of supply chain management.

SUMMARY

We use several conventions in this book. Purchasing is moving away from a transactional and product based model to an integrated supply process model. The integrated process model is called supply chain management. Buyers or agents are called supply managers. In much the same way, supply chain management is simplified to supply management. We also abbreviate Supply Chain Management to SCM.

The name of the department or function where SCM resides is called purchasing, sourcing, or supply management. We refer to the new purchasing function as supply management. This is consistent with the Institute of Supply Management.

We believe in continuous improvement. If you have any comments on how to improve this book, please call us at 800.COMPETE (800.266.7383). We want this to be the best supply chain product around. Thank you for buying this book.

Greg Hutchins, PE
Quality Plus Engineering
Working It, LLC
Portland, Oregon

CHAPTER 2: COMPETITIVENESS FUNDAMENTALS

Capitalism, competitiveness, dot.com profitability, disruption, and innovation are today's paradigm busters. They are what drive today's New Economy. Capitalism is triumphant in almost every activity in every corner of the world. National boundaries are disappearing as goods and services move freely. Competitiveness and innovation are continually destroying the current business paradigm. Just as a business feels it has found its niche and understands what is going on, supply management and sourcing rules change again.

COMPETITIVENESS - TODAY'S PARADIGM BUSTER

There is no finish line.
Nike Corporation motto

The President's report several years ago defined national competitiveness as:

> "Competitiveness for a nation is the degree to which it can, under free and fair market conditions, produce goods and services that meet the test of international markets while simultaneously maintaining and expanding the real incomes of its citizens. Competitiveness is the basis for a nation's standard of living".[1]

COMPETITIVE TRANSFORMATIONS

Supply management is fundamentally a competitive transformation, much like reengineering. Business transformations follow a value and process based approach to change. Names and fads may change but the evolution is the same. As a result of competitive pressures, companies question what they are doing, why they are doing it, and how they can do it better. Nowadays, entire industry sectors are transformed by competitive pressures. Typical transformations initiatives include:

US Auto Industry Wake Up Call

General Motors, once America's most innovative company, developed a reputation for me-too, unimaginative cars through much of the 1980s and 1990s. The Japanese were eating GM's lunch specifically through better-designed, higher quality, and higher value vehicles. The results were disastrous. GM's U.S. market share plummeted. GM got the message and its quality ratings are now the highest of U.S. automakers.

Bank Transformations

Banking changes almost weekly. Customers want high quality, personal service at the lowest possible cost. Customers want banks to be open when they are needed such as after five pm on workdays and open on Saturdays. Many banks first enhanced their service delivery based on traditional bank mindsets. That didn't work well. Another layer of cost and customer service management was created. Senior bank officials realized they must fundamentally change how they operated so ATMs were installed to provide 24-hour customer service.

COMPETITIVE PRINCIPLES

Most of the companies that rated among the top 100 today were not there 20 or even 10 years ago and some had not even started.
Anonymous

Supply managers must know the rules of the competitiveness game. Our employers, internal customers, and suppliers base their business decisions on competitiveness rules that affect each of us, specifically:

CONTEXT: Competitive Commandments of the 21st Century

- Don't play by the dominant competitive rules of an industry.
- Get innovative or get dead.
- Reexamine a company's hidden strategic assets, then leverage the hell out of them.
- Create a bias for speed and action.
- Be proactive and experimental.
- Break down barriers.
- Use all people's skills all the time.
- Globalize the company's perspective and knowledge base.
- Admit the eco-industrial revolution is well and truly upon us.
- Turn organizational learning into a corporate religion.
- Develop strategic performance measurement tools.[2]

There is no commonly accepted list of SCM principles and assumptions. It seems every supply chain guru and consultant have his or her own set of beliefs. The following are generally accepted SCM principles and are introduced throughout this book:

- **Competition is global and fierce.** This decade will focus on international competitiveness. SCM is a critical means to position a company, its products, and services for continued profitability.

- **Competitively priced, high value products and services sell.** Studies assert that real and perceived value in brands, products, and services sell. In industrial, commercial, and consumer buy decisions, value is either the top criterion for making the buy decision or near the top along with cost, delivery, and service.

- **Sales produce profits and jobs.** If high value products and services sell at sufficient profit margins, they should generate continued profits for the organization and its supply chain. Profits ensure jobs.

- **'Make or buy' decision.** If a company has core process capabilities or core competencies then it will make the product. If it does not, then it will buy (source) the product from 'world class' suppliers with complementary core process competencies.

- **Total customer satisfaction produces sales.** Total customer satisfaction and value production are the goals of all stakeholders including management, suppliers, employees, stockholders, community and the supply chain. Total customer satisfaction means every customer experience is positive and pleasing so the result is a repeat customer. Total customer satisfaction is achieved through managing controllable value factors, such as managing supply cycle time, quality, communications, risk, technology, and performance.

- **'Voice of the customer' is internalized.** 'Voice of the customer' is internalized and deployed throughout the supply chain.

- **Total customer satisfaction is facilitated through SCM.** SCM focuses all stakeholders on satisfying customer requirements.

- **SCM is a strategic business issue.** SCM matures to become part of an organization's critical mission as a company determines its product mix based on blended internal capabilities and supply-partner core capabilities.

- **Partnering with 'world class' suppliers.** The outsourcing decision goes something like this. If a customer understands a supplier has the same business model and ethic as it does then both can synergize their distinct core competencies.

- **Cycle time, JIT, lean, quality, benchmarking, and logistics management are basic to SCM.** Fundamental to all SCM activities is the need to continuously improve, be lean, and have JIT processes. Basically, what was good enough yesterday isn't sufficient for guaranteeing tomorrow's profitability. Continuous improvement is pursued throughout the supply chain. Suppliers must improve their capability and move up a process maturity curve.

- **Auditing, corrective action, and preventive action close the improvement loop.** Systems, processes, and product are audited. If there are nonconformances or deficiencies, corrective action eliminates their root cause and preventive action prevents their recurrence.

- **SCM relies on self-management and self-initiative.** SCM requires supply chain stakeholders to identify problems, identify risks, intervene when necessary, develop solutions, eliminate the symptom, and root cause of the problem.

- **Critical SCM systems, process and product parameters are continuously measured.** To achieve performance benchmarks, key supply process variables are measured inside the organization and with key suppliers. The measurements of customer requirements become the metrics or milestones in the SCM journey.

- **All forms of waste are eliminated.** A key SCM objective is to become lean through eliminating waste. Waste can be excess materials, inefficiencies, redundancies, poor service, duplication of efforts, or high cost.

- **All SCM stakeholders are empowered to improve.** Responsibility and authority for SCM activities are pushed down to the lowest organizational level and to the appropriate suppliers.

- **People are cross-trained and compensated for learning.** Continuous and breakthrough improvement requires continuous supply development to keep up with changing customer requirements, trends, and technology.

- **Need for competitiveness, value, and innovation drives all business decisions, actions, and product development.** Competitiveness is now part of every supply chain's vision, mission, and plans. Competitiveness drives the need for change and product innovation.

SUMMARY

The world has become an international marketplace. In this marketplace, products from Europe, the Pacific Rim, and South and North America compete for the customer's buying dollar. The money spent on a product by a customer means the company that produced the product or the supply chain that delivered the product will have the capital to maintain and expand its operations. It also means the company will keep its people employed making more products to sell in the international marketplace.

A number of factors, some would say opportunities and risks are increasing the importance of supply management. These factors include a global economy, customer demand changes, low-price competition, environmentalism, consumerism, technological changes, and product lifecycle reduction.

Occurring simultaneously, customers are demanding high quality products and services that are delivered quickly and courteously. As well, products and services are tailored to satisfy national and local requirements. Time to market becomes a critical success factor. Medtronic, maker of half of the world's pacemakers, has a full 50% of its revenues coming from products introduced over the past 12 months.[3]

CHAPTER 3:
SUPPLY CHAIN MANAGEMENT

Each company should have a set of core capabilities, in other words something that the company is exceptionally good at. The company can use its core capabilities to distinguish itself to customers or to differentiate itself from competitors. For example, Volvo develops innovative and safe autos, Wal-Mart has a super efficient supply management system, and Nordstrom offers exceptional customer service in the apparel trades.

HUTCHINS'S RULES OF GLOBAL BUSINESS

One way to increase productivity is to do whatever we are doing now, but faster ... there is a second way. We can change the nature of the work we do, not how fast we do it.
Andrew Grove, CEO Intel

Several years ago, I was asked to distill the rules of global business. I facetiously called them: 'Hutchins's Rules of Global Business.' The major points were:

- Please your stakeholders.

- Identify what you do best.

- Institutionalize core processes.

- Outsource noncore work to 'world class' suppliers.

- Acquire supply processes as well as products.

- Measure supply performance.

- Innovate and improve continuously.

Let us explore each one:

PLEASE YOUR STAKEHOLDERS

Since Tom Peters wrote his opus **In Search of Excellence**, pleasing the customer has been a conventional wisdom of business excellence. The customer was first considered the external customer, the final user; then the concept was enlarged to include the internal customer, the person next in line adding product value. We thus could see the beginning of the supply chain concept. Then the supply chain definition expanded to include all customer-supply links.

The final customer is only one of a growing number of *internal* supply chain stakeholders that must be satisfied in a global economy. A customer may also be part of the *external* supply chain links, which may include local authorities, state government, or federal government. More and more, regulatory authorities, dealing with safety, environmental, consumer and health issues, are growing in importance. Therefore, a partial list of SCM stakeholders would include final and internal customers, management and employees, distributors, shareholders, government, suppliers, and unions.

As we enter the new millennium, satisfying if not pleasing these stakeholders becomes more important. It almost may be said that any of these stakeholders may have veto power for a company to enter new markets, be profitable, and even survive.

IDENTIFY WHAT YOU DO BEST

A company can't be all things to all people. An organization must focus on what it does best. In a competitive economy, the goal is to become 'world class' - the best in a market in one or several key processes. Best can be in terms of designing widgets, supplying typing services, providing legal work, assembling printed circuit boards, or sourcing products. Best requires that a company discover and focus on its core process competencies. To become the best in supply management requires simplicity, lean thinking/doing, risk management, and control of supply chain.

As large companies attempted to please customers with a large variety of products, several problems arose. Products would have different features, performance or external aesthetics. Large plants would be built with parallel management, design, production, marketing and distribution systems. Overlapping systems created increased variation, miscommunication, unbalanced flows, system constraints, and redundancies that inevitably resulted in confusion. Bureaucracies were built that tended to protect turf instead of pleasing the customer. All of which are anathema to a lean and integrated supply chain.

As well, no company ultimately has the ability to be the best in each business area. Being the best requires an abundance of resources that no organization has. What often occurs is that resources are spread too thin and the organization does many things only moderately well.

INSTITUTIONALIZE CORE PROCESSES

Core processes are essential to the operation and success of any business. Core processes are often horizontal and multifunctional spanning different functions, plants, and departments throughout the organization. For example, supply chain core competencies may involve engineering that develops robust drawings and accurate bills of material; involve production that has special handling, delivery, or packaging abilities; involve quality that conducts special testing and supplier audits; and involve accounting that ensures timely accounts payable and accounts receivable. The supply management function links these disparate activities into an integrated core process.

Often a company may only have one strategic area of excellence, internal capability, or core competency, which may involve supply chain management, low costs, state-of-the-art research and development, critical management abilities, special equipment, quality culture, team effectiveness, technology/know-how, or distribution strengths.[1] More companies now view supply chain management or strategic sourcing as a core competency to be developed.

A good business case can be made for focusing on core process competencies. J.P. Morgan, the investment bank, concluded that American companies that focused on the one thing they did well outperformed the stock market by 11% while diversified companies underperformed the market by 4%.[2]

OUTSOURCE NONCORE WORK TO 'WORLD-CLASS' SUPPLIERS

The rationale for outsourcing goes something like this. We, the manufacturer, are in the business of making widgets so why should we spend our time focusing on running our own telephone company, information technology department, or training organization. The company should spend its time on things that will make a real difference to the customer, impact the bottom line and leverage its core competencies.[3]

The process of outsourcing non-core work is called virtual work, dis-integration, or strategic sourcing. The result is the same. Companies focus on core activities and outsource all other work. This is occurring in a major way. Lucent Technology handed off $8 billion of its manufacturing to outside suppliers. Cisco outsourced all of its subassembly manufacturing and 42% of its final assembly of its routers and switches. Nearly 80% of Kodak's reloadable cameras and all of its digital cameras are sourced in Asia.[4]

Customer-Supply Partnering

Vertical integration is losing its appeal to new forms of cooperation, co-ordination and communication involving supply-partners. Global competition, high product development costs, high quality expectations, low cost requirements, shortened product life cycles, and individual customer requirements are accelerating the change to customer-supply integration and partnering.

Supply-partners are expected to be very good at what they do; in other words to be 'world class.' More often, work is sourced to a single supply-partner and/or acceptable alternate supplier for each product line. The rationale for selecting two suppliers is that one supplier may not change quickly, continuously innovate, and continuously lower costs. As well, the customer assumes inordinate risk with one supplier in terms of an act of God, strike, or other unforeseeable event stopping shipments.

Often, supply-partners are nimble entrepreneurs that know local customer requirements, have access to global information, and are monomaniacal in the pursuit of pleasing the customer. Flexibility, quickness, and actions are the code words of their success.

This is happening worldwide. Many Japanese firms form keiretsus, which are formal financial, engineering, manufacturing and supply networks. Japanese transplants are importing this model to the U.S. While still new in the U.S., these relationships are characterized by close product development partnerships. Cost, design, delivery, customer service, and proprietary information are commonly shared. The hoped-for results are minimized variation, eliminated redundancies, enhanced communications, and improved co-ordination.

ACQUIRE SUPPLY PROCESSES AS WELL AS PRODUCTS

Many purchasing professionals still focus on the transaction, buying products instead of securing reliable supplier processes and systems. This requires a shift of thinking, moving away from simply buying products to securing a reliable source with robust, stable, and capable processes. If the means by which a product or service is produced is reliable then the outcome will meet contractual requirements, surpass customer expectations, and ultimately add value.

Modern supply management assumes if customer requirements are understood and internalized, then supply-partners have the systems and processes in place to address these requirements. If these processes are controlled and improved, then there is a high level of assurance the products or services coming out of these processes satisfy customer expectations.

MEASURE SUPPLY PERFORMANCE

How is 'world class' determined? Supplier performance throughout the contract or product lifecycle is continuously monitored. Traditionally, commercial buy decisions were based on price, availability, and delivery. Similarly, consumer buy decisions were largely based on price and packaging. Now industrial and commercial buy decisions are more complex, based on verifiable quality, total cost, eye-catching design, environmental friendliness, and other factors.

While consumer decisions are often the result of on-the-spot visceral responses, most industrial and commercial buy decisions are based on well thought out, researched analysis. Suppliers may even be certified or registered to some standard, such as ISO 9001: 2015.

INNOVATE AND IMPROVE CONTINUOUSLY

Standing still in a fast-moving economic stream is the equivalent of moving backwards. Treading water is death in high-tech markets. The obvious solution is to innovate and improve continuously. Innovation is the ability to conceptualize and commercialize new products. Improvement is the ability to control and minimize process variation so there are few defective products.

Theoretically if a company builds on its strengths, it will consistently achieve competitive returns from its business. Customers will flock to it because of its distinguishing characteristics, abilities, products, or services. A cohesive mission, strategies, and objectives allow business units, suppliers, plants, teams, and processes to be linked and synergized. The challenge for the new supply manager is to develop, nurture, evoke, and reinforce these unique characteristics throughout the supply chain.

WHAT IS SUPPLY CHAIN MANAGEMENT?

An airplane is a system of spare parts flying in close formation.
Orville Wright

One of the powerful analytical tools in management theory is the systems approach, which explains complex relationships in simple terms. A system is a group of elements or processes that function together to achieve a common goal. Elements can be parts of an organization, including suppliers, distributors, and other parties.

SUPPLY CHAIN IS A SYSTEM

This book presents a systems approach to supply chain management where independent and interdependent supply elements and processes work together to deliver quality products and services that satisfy customer wants, needs, and expectations.

David Anders, Frank Britt, and Donavon in **The Seven Principles of Supply Chain Management** offered the following systems wisdom to supply managers:

> "These savvy (supply) managers recognized two important things. First they think about the supply chain as a whole – all the links involved in managing the flow of products, services, and information from their suppliers' suppliers to their customers' customers (that is channel customers, such as distributors and retailers). Second, they pursue tangible outcomes – focused on revenue growth, asset utilization, and cost reduction."[5]

WHAT IS A SUPPLY CHAIN?

There is no universally accepted definition of a 'supply chain.' APICS, the Educational Society for Resource Management, has one of the better definitions and defines 'supply chain' as:

> "The processes from the initial raw materials to the ultimate consumption of the finished product linking across supplier-user

companies. The functions inside and outside a company that enable the value chain to make products and provide services to the customer."[6]

And, other definitions are:

"A group of companies connected loosely, all collaborating on the same goal: efficient and economical product delivery. Or, the set of order-entry and order-fulfillment-related physical interactions connecting a company and its customers and suppliers."[7]

"Supply chain management considers the management of materials and products from suppliers through all internal operations, including distribution to the customer. It's designed to:

- Optimize network and material flow.

- Reduce costs and cash consumption.

- Increase speed.

- Streamline, align, and focus information flow.

- Streamline and refocus the organization from functional and national to process and cross-border".[8]

SERIES OF SUPPLY PROCESS CHAINS

The fulfillment of orders is really a series of process chains that operate simultaneously. At the broadest level, the supply chain consists of all the processes and activities to deliver a product from the field to the dinner table or from the mine to the worktable.

At another level, the supply process chain includes all the activities involved in producing, storing, and delivering manufactured goods to their ultimate destination. It originates at the enterprise level and flows towards the customer.

So, the scope of SCM often depends on the perspective of the user. Does the supply chain include all suppliers of all products and services throughout the product lifecycle from customer needs assessment to product definition to final delivery? Or, does the supply chain include only critical suppliers one level deep in each supply chain?

The integrated supply chain extends well beyond first-tier suppliers to include sub tier suppliers, transportation, warehousing, manufacturing, engineering, and customers. This makes it difficult to manage so the chain is more often defined or scoped to the 'critical few' supply-partners.

MAKING A BUSINESS CASE FOR SUPPLY CHAIN MANAGEMENT

Ian Stewart and David McCutcheon in **Manager's Guide to Supply Chain Management** made the case for strategic outsourcing:

> "The strategic objectives in outsourcing an input are relatively straightforward. Basically, firms are interested in how they can either significantly reduce product costs or add to what customers perceive as value-added benefits. Naturally, firms hope that the value-added benefits can be achieved at lower cost, but in such cases the cost role is subordinate. Value-added benefits might include improved delivery speed, additional design features and options, or the ability to be customized. Some of these benefits are best achieved by using in-house product design and process management capabilities."[9]

> "Firms continue to identify core competencies, seeking the inherent benefits - such as improved knowledge depth and organizational learning - of greater focus. Other specific technologies may be essential for competitiveness but it may not be practical to maintain expertise for them in-house. The science base may be changing too rapidly, making it risky to be a player in that field. Or, it may be too expensive to maintain technological competence. Or, the product may be too complex for any firm to manage all aspects internally. In each case, outsourcing the

---

CONTEXT: Competitive Organizations Ask!

- Does the organization focus on its core competencies or out-source the work to supply-partners?
- What are the risks and value to each group?
- Are the right suppliers working on the right things?
- Are suppliers induced and compensated in the most appropriate ways?
- Are they supplied the appropriate information to get the job done?
- Is the supply chain organized and managed in the most efficient, effective, and economic manner?

---

technology becomes an alternative, but one that entails risks, especially if suppliers provide critical proprietary capabilities and technology integration skills."[10]

SHIFTING PARADIGMS

Business is war!
Jack Tramiel, CEO

Paradigm (pronounced pair-a-dime) has become a cliché. Joel Barker in **Paradigms: The Business of Discovering the Future** defines a paradigm as:

> "…a set of rules and regulations (written or unwritten) that does two things: 1. it establishes or defines boundaries; and 2. it tells you how to behave inside the boundaries in order to be successful."[11]

The word 'paradigm' comes from the Greek and means a pattern or model. A paradigm is the way people perceives their world. It can mean a world of difference. Fish perceive their world through water. We perceive our world through air. Supply managers perceive their world through supply links in an integrated process chain.

Often, paradigms are defined in terms of a game. A game has a set of rules, which players must follow. The game often has boundaries such as a racquetball court, baseball park, or supply chain. The game also requires specific skills to compete. A professional baseball player runs bases, hits a curveball, fastball, slider, and fields a ball. Players keep score. The game score defines winners and losers. In much the same way, SCM is a game with rules, which we discuss later in this book.

PARADIGM SHIFTS

A paradigm shift is a sudden and dramatic change in game rules. Paradigm shifts can be monumental or small. Usually, small shifts serve as a precursor to larger changes. What was right before may now be wrong. What was the pathway to success may no longer be the case. For example, law may now expressly forbid what was acceptable workplace behavior five years ago.

Paradigm shifts are difficult for supply managers who were hired, taught, recognized, promoted, and reinforced for a set of behaviors and activities that are now either unacceptable or have radically changed. This has happened in many traditional purchasing, materials management, design, manufacturing, and planning functions within companies and in supply bases.

A paradigm shift was thought to occur in select areas or functions once in a lifetime. Now, change is so dramatic it has become the norm instead of the rare occurrence. It's happening in business, regulations, professions, and technology. One way to manage change is to understand supply management rules and boundary conditions.

Even in this new supply chain game, there are some fixed rules, fundamentals and boundaries. No matter how many balls, strikes, or bases, players still have to run, throw, catch, and swing. And even in a game with floating rules, some organizations can create winning competitive strategies focused on the supply chain fundamentals covered in this book.

SUPPLY CHAIN PARADIGM SHIFT

The change from purchasing to supply management is a paradigm shift. As discussed, paradigm shifts occur when the fundamentals and assumptions of a process, discipline or work change overnight. We can fairly well say the purchasing function, as we knew it ten years ago has seen a paradigm shift.

Supply chain management is sometimes described in terms of the following set of changing rules, boundary conditions, tools, and expectations:

- **Set of rules.** Most written and implicit purchasing rules have changed in the last twenty years. Much of this is due to changes in technology and the rise of ecommerce.

- **Boundary conditions.** Until a few years ago, the boundary conditions for almost all purchasing involved the customer-supply transaction. Now, it involves the entire supply value chain. And, the supply chain simultaneously is becoming more global and virtual.

- **Tools.** The tools of the buyer or agent only a few years ago were pencils, pens, and mechanical devices. Now, supply management tools are electronic including faxes, cell phones, laptop computers linked via e-commerce Intranets, ERPs, CRMs, and the Internet.

- **Expectations.** A buyer entering the purchasing workplace twenty or even ten years ago assumed lifetime loyalty was rewarded with lifetime employment. In much the same way, suppliers entering into a business relationship with a customer expected long term, reliable margins. No longer! Like employees, suppliers expect their contract to be in place as long as they offer value-adding capabilities and processes. Traditional supply loyalty to the customer was rewarded with a long-term contract. Now rewards are based on cost, quality, delivery, and technology improvement.[12]

SUPPLY CHAIN BENEFITS

Consumers are getting smarter. They will shop for the best buy, will pay for only what they really want, and will switch products or service suppliers in a heartbeat. What does this mean for the supply chain? More change and uncertainty create opportunities to distinguish a supply chain from its competition.

Outsourcing systems and subassemblies to a capable supply chain can be a major asset for the following reasons. First tier suppliers assume responsibility for meeting specifications on a turnkey basis. Sometimes, second-tier or lower level suppliers are non-union shops where the costs of rework and scrap are typically lower than in-house assembly workers. Finally, outsourcing the subassembly makes for a cleaner and less cluttered assembly space where the subassembly is bolted on or fixed onto the final products. This helps reduce in-house cycle times.

THE VIRTUAL BUSINESS MODEL

Manage the opportunities change offers.
Advertisement.

Some companies are going to extremes to focus on core competencies by 'virtualizing' most or all of their business. Remember when companies made things? In the future, some companies may end up with few hard assets. Their core assets will be intellectual capital: trademarks, brands, people, inspiration, knowledge, or a supply chain business model. This is already practiced in software, consulting, and legal services. A company's work will consist of core process workers and special project workers who feed the core processes. This cannibalization or hollowing out of a business is sometimes called 'brand management.'

CONTEXT: Supply Management Trends

- Businesses outsource more. Companies are building less themselves and making supply management a key driver of profitability.
- Businesses and their supply webs become increasingly virtual. Each new product development cycle requires developing a new supply chain to meet market needs and then disassembling it when needs have been met.
- Competitiveness is the fundamental business driver. Globalization of the economy forces all businesses to be more competitive.
- Customers keep getting smarter, demanding more. They become highly sensitive to costs, delivery speeds, technology innovation and service levels.
- Customers demand mass customization. They want specific features and functionality in the products they buy.
- Technology becomes cheaper. Technology and communications become cheaper.
- Companies use technology to standardize decision processes. Technology also links all decision-making to profitability measures. Decisions that may impact business profits are scrutinized more closely.
- Companies continue to lower permanent staffing levels. Rising competitive pressures demand improved skill sets from a smaller group of supply management professionals.
- Availability of mountains of data facilitates smarter decision-making. Companies have accurate data to support decision making internally and throughout the supply chain.
- Internet-based and ecommerce technologies collapse physical distances. This accelerates the transition to a truly global economy.[13]

VIRTUAL BUSINESS

This virtual business model is predicated on an effective and efficient supply chain. Some companies are transforming their supply base into a virtual supply chain enabled by the Internet. The key driving factors for this include the need to decrease cycle times, increase operating flexibility and reduce total supply chain costs. To achieve this, critical supply chain partners must identify and focus on their core competencies.

Look at some virtualizing of business:

Sara Lee Corporation

Sara Lee Corporation sold its noncore factories. It focused on its core strengths, specifically developing new products, managing its brands, and increasing market share. Sara Lee outsourced commodity manufacturing and other noncore activities and only retained its 'highly proprietary' processes. In other words, it focused on 'what it did best.'[14]

British Airlines

Even airlines are becoming virtual because of competition and deregulation. British Airways cut it costs and increased operational flexibility leasing its air fleet by the month, leasing aircraft engines by the hour, and hired outside pilots and mechanics.

The airline looked to suppliers to provide everything from spare parts to routine maintenance to flight training. The airline envisioned it would supply little more than its brand name and its schedule. This could be a problem with regulators who worry about safety and from passengers who put their trust in big name airplane brands.[15]

Amazon.com

Amazon.com reinvents itself and changes its business model almost yearly. Amazon.com is the poster company of the 'New Economy' and for most e-business. Amazon.com started as an online bookseller but has morphed into a purveyor of new goods and services.

In its latest incarnation, its core business is to collect customer buying information and then pull this information together into individual customer profiles. These are used to promote and sell unrelated products such as toys, electronics, books, and videos to specific customers. This type of virtual business morphs based on market conditions and customer requirements. Its core business is no longer a product or service, but a business model.[16]

Information Technology

Information technology is one function that lends itself to massive outsourcing. Hilton Hotels farmed out the lion's share of its $12 million information technology (IT) budget to two vendors. General Dynamics spun off most of its entire 2,500 person IT organization in 1991 so it could morph from a lumbering defense contractor into a nimble commercial enterprise. General Dynamics in the process shrunk from a $10 billion to a $3 billion a year company.

One virtual computer company hired other companies to design and build all its computers, answer repair questions, invoice bills, and ship products. The only thing it does is sell and maintains its brand.

The Auto Industry

The auto industry already outsources up to 70% of its manufacturing to suppliers, but now we are seeing auto companies outsource most of their noncore processes.

VALUE CHAIN AS A CORE COMPETENCY

The company with the second best organization ends up second place in the market.
D. Wayne Calloway, CEO PepsiCo, Inc.

Core processes generate value through innovation, uniqueness, and flexibility. The supply chain is a value chain based on an overall process from the smallest supplier up the tiers to the deliverer of the product to the customer. And within each company, there are many subprocesses that link or feed the overall supply chain process.

SUPPLY CHAIN = VALUE CHAIN

In simplest terms, a value chain is the entire design-production-delivery-service process, regardless of which firm owns any particular value-adding step. The value chain encompasses not only first-tier suppliers but suppliers' suppliers, but also customers and the customers' customers as well.[17] The value chain integrates the core processes to provide a seamless chain of value adding opportunities.

Adding value and eliminating value detractors are fundamental SCM objectives. Value is the real and perceived utility a customer or user has in a product or service. To add customer value or utility means that a feature has been added or performance has been improved so the product's image is enhanced and the product is more marketable. Supply management can be thought as a managing seven value-related factors:

Form Value
Form value is the aesthetic, external features of a product. It should be added that a product consists of tangible and intangible elements. Depending on the nature of the product, such as a fashion or consumer product, form may be the most important value attribute.

Time Value
Time value means reducing cycle times throughout the supply chain from product development to delivery. More often, time value is associated with having the product available when the customer wants it. This is important to suppliers of manufacturing companies. Firms don't want a large inventory on their books because it's expensive. Today, the goal is to keep all costs low, including the cost of carrying inventory. Firms now ask suppliers to provide products just-in-time to be used or assembled into a finished product.

Cost Value
Cost value is the overall cost of the product or service over the contract or product lifecycle. Transactional purchasing traditionally dealt with the price of the delivered product at one point in time. Part of the partnering assumption is the customer will invest time, resources, and technology with supply-partners who will share cost reductions with the customer.

CONTEXT: Supply Chain Assumptions

- All work is a process.
- Each process has inputs and outputs.
- Each process has a supplier(s) and customer(s).
- Each process can be controlled, made consistent, and improved.
- Each process and each process step adds value.
- Quality, service, delivery, service, performance, efficiency and economics are measured.
- Each process can be documented and measured.
- If the process works as intended, the outputs should conform to customer requirements.

Information Value

Information value is the ability to have the right information at the right time to make smart decisions. Information value requires the right technology infrastructure and empowered professionals to make decisions.

Place Value

Place value means having products available where the customer wants it or in other words, managing logistics. In the preceding JIT production example, manufacturers want parts delivered directly to the location on the manufacturing line where they will be used. For example, an industrial customer may ask a supplier to deliver parts to loading dock No.10 at 9:00 am on December 6th in Portland, Oregon so they can be assembled onto the finished part.

Possession Value

Possession value means completing the transaction and gaining possession so the customer has the legal right to use the product. Information, warranties, spare parts, and instructions have been provided to the customer so he or she can use the product safely.

Perceived Value

Perceived value is the overall perception of a product or service. Often, this involves intangible product and service attributes. Positive perceptions of a supplier may result from its brand, service, quality reputation, supplier reputation, product design, and the many little things that create perceptions.[18]

HOW THE SUPPLY CHAIN ADDS VALUE

The real issue is value, not price.
Robert Lindgren, Business person

An important element of supply management isn't to look at sourcing at a transaction level but at a process or relationship level. The long-term goal is to establish mutually beneficial relationships. Sourcing isn't an end in itself but a means to establish a supply chain, which brings end-to-end value.

HOW TO ADD INNOVATION VALUE

More industrial and commercial supply managers as well as consumers are buying based on real and perceived value. According to Mike Treacy and Fred Wiersma in **The Discipline of Market Leaders**, competitive companies identify value added characteristics, features, or services that customers really want and then raise customer expectations in one or two areas of value. Every competitor entering the market is then judged by the market leader's delivery of value. In other words, a company or a person has three value strategies: follow the leader, break out of the pack, or move ahead of the pack.

According to Treacy and Wiersma, the innovative company competes on one of three value disciplines, specifically on:

- **Operational value.** Operationally excellent companies offer middle-of-the-market products at a competitive price with the least convenience.

- **Product leadership.** Product-leader companies offer products that push performance and value boundaries.

- **Customer intimacy.** Customer-intimate companies deliver product and service value that satisfy specific customer needs.

While a company may perform well in many areas, following the competitiveness precept of 'stick to your knitting,' companies will develop and focus on a few core competence strategies.

ADDING SUPPLY CHAIN VALUE

Value is the most critical element to process improvement and supply chain management. Value, the opposite of cost or waste, is the only true measure of determining whether a function, activity, or process is providing customer satisfaction, efficiency, effectiveness, or other performance benefits.

Conventional business wisdom now says product quality by itself isn't enough to please customers. Now, it must be the right bundle of price-competitive, products and services delivered just in time and in the right manner to the customer. In other words, value incorporates form, time, cost, and the other value elements discussed in the prior section.

SCM value can be added by:

- Increasing features.

- Cutting costs.

- Technology enhancements.

- Bundling.

Add Value By Increasing Features

Suppliers can add product features, increase performance, or personalize a product to enhance product value. Manufacturers may offer a basic line of automobiles or may offer limited editions with special performance packages to attract upscale consumers. For example to update a well-known automobile, one manufacturer added features, increased engine performance, changed its name and image, and charged a premium price.

Add Value By Cutting Costs

One supply management truism is to 'drive unnecessary costs out of the system and return them to the customer.' The evidence is all around us. Post Raisin Bran dropped from $4.13 to $2.99 for a 20-ounce box. Sprint's off peak, long distance telephone calls averaged 15.4 cents a minute two years ago and now costs less than 10 cents a minute. A product's price/value can be reduced through increasing internal efficiencies and lowering operational costs.

In the supply chain, customers and suppliers are collaborating to provide higher value. Companies are communicating this to all supply chain stakeholders including employees. Employees, even in traditionally adversarial work environments, partner with management to make companies cost competitive. Ford Motor Company asked its employees, United Auto Workers, to find ways to cut costs in the new Taurus. Savings came in small increments but mounted. The goal was to make the car competitive in the cutthroat, midsize sedan market by allowing the company to raise profits by holding down price increases and offering bigger discounts.[19]

Add Value Through Technology Enhancements

Value can also be added through redesigning a product such as an automobile and collaborating with key suppliers during the development process. Let us look at how vehicles have changed. Fins, chrome, straight lines, curved lines come in and out of design fashion. The jellybean auto look that dominated most of the 80s and 90s is officially dead. The new Mustangs have a hard-edged look that is decidedly different from the soft, sweeping lines found several years ago when the car was redesigned. The Japanese and Germans are also following this automotive lead.[20]

CONTEXT: Supply Chain Tips

- **Plan long-term**. Critical supply chain factors such as inventory and time-to-market will vary within the product life cycle. Make sure to choose a product, and set up a solution, that can accommodate to change throughout the product lifecycle.
- **Ensure short-term results.** Supply management projects should be short and demonstrate results that matter.
- **Qualify suppliers.** Eliminate suppliers with inventory and customer service problems.
- **Focus on one piece of the supply chain puzzle at a time.** There are many elements, links, and activities in a supply chain. A company is probably part of someone's supply chain as well as has its own supply chain. Focus on the part of the puzzle with the greatest impact. Remember the Pareto principle (80-20 rule).
- **Partner with or hire logistics talent.** Supply chain solutions require specialized knowledge and assistance. Invest in getting and institutionalizing specialized knowledge and skills.
- **Don't underestimate the difficulty of connecting to a host or other computer systems.** Supply chain solutions usually integrate many platforms, including legacy systems.
- **Consider the wider SCM community.** Supply chain solutions affect customers, suppliers and freight companies. Make sure communication lines are open and that everyone understands SCM goals and deliverables.
- **Source multiple suppliers if there are risks.** Don't put all your eggs in one basket. Diversify supply chain risks.
- **Focus on training.** SCM users must be educated on new SCM metrics and trained how to use them to achieve business goals.
- **Develop suppliers carefully.** Look for and integrate cutting-edge, synergistic supplier competencies.[21]

Add Value By Bundling

Manufacturers and service providers can add value by bundling services and products to provide the customer with additional value. For example, Starbucks is the company that got us to spring for a $4 or $5 exotic cup of coffee. Now, it's moving to sandwiches, salads and other 'grab-and-go' foods. Café Starbucks will probably be popping up in your favorite coffee shop or as a stand-alone restaurant. What is going on? Starbucks wants to turn its caffeinated brand name into a lifestyle.

INFORMATION IS POWER

In the New Economy, core knowledge and innovative information may evolve into the distinguishing competitive feature of the supply chain. In the e-commerce world, the supply chain is now a web. Many of today's supply chain gurus argue that e-commerce and Internet are all about making communication powerful and information cheap.

Information is power. The people who have the right information have a business advantage and the opportunity to make money. This applies to supply chains, organizations, and people. If a company has a killer new idea then it can increase economies of scale by sharing it with supply chain partners. The Internet and ecommerce ensure that reliable, timely, and valuable information is available to everyone.[22]

SUMMARY

Competitiveness, pleasing customers, and adding value drive all business decisions. Today's rules of competitiveness come down to a few common sense tips: know what you do best, focus on these core process competencies and outsource all other work. It sounds pretty simple but its execution is profoundly difficult. **In Blown to Bits**, Philip Evan and Thomas Wurster argue that every business will have to pick apart the processes that lie behind their products and put their value chain back together in different ways.

Value addition and elimination of value detractors/inhibitors are now critical for survival and long-term success. These are the fundamental success drivers of the supply chain.

CHAPTER 4:
CUSTOMER FOCUS

Supply chain management starts with a customer focus. Companies know that it costs three to five times as much to find a new customer as it does to retain a customer. Customer satisfaction and customer loyalty now drive all SCM initiatives. The *Economist Magazine* said:

> "... companies are stumbling to find new ways to manage their relationships with their customers. ... Only happy customers will be loyal ones – and loyalty is something companies desperately need if they are to survive in today's difficult economic climate."[1]

CUSTOMER RELATIONSHIP MANAGEMENT

Be everywhere, do everything, and never fail to astonish the customer.
Margaret Getchell

Customer relationship management (CRM) is the flip side of supply chain management (SCM). The logic goes something like this. Every company is market oriented. What does that mean? Market or customer oriented companies deliver cost-competitive quality products or services. Supply chain processes target specific or mass market segments with defined and coordinated market strategies. The supply chain challenge is now to induce entrepreneurial customer-supply chains to work cohesively under a unifying customer-focused strategy.

CUSTOMER RELATIONSHIP MANAGEMENT

Companies are differentiating themselves from the competition by knowing customer wants and satisfying these wants. Amazon.com, eBay and other companies are assembling massive amounts of information on customer preferences based on surveys, buying patterns, etc. The Ritz Carlton developed a detailed database of a customer's past visits so front desk personnel can anticipate requirements. Their aim is to know what people buy so they can sell services directly to people based on these preferences.

Customer specific purchasing profiles are common in retail credit card purchasing. Most retail and consumer products are now bar coded and scanned. Let us look at the process. The retail person scans the product. Package labels/codes are tied to a company's sales number in the retailer's system and a receipt is printed for the consumer. This point of sale (POS) data is connected with the credit card name and is used to develop customer profiles. The POS data is then sent to a market databank to generate and store customer personal purchasing. And, the data is sent to suppliers to create tailored replenishment data based on buying patterns.

UNDERSTAND CUSTOMER REQUIREMENTS

The supply chain starts with identifying customer requirements and ends by developing and delivering the right products on time to the customer. The customer may be an industrial buyer, commercial buyer, or consumer. It's critical that all supply chain initiatives, projects, and activities emphasize customer priorities and develop strategies on how to satisfy them. Supply management's responsibility is to integrate the organization's core process competencies with the supply base competencies to enhance customer satisfaction.

The problem is too many companies and by inference supply chains are still managed by priorities and politics that don't matter to the customer or that generate no income. Too many SCM improvement and performance initiatives tend to focus on criteria that are not important to the customer. Too many companies have discovered that feature-rich, user-unfriendly, high-tech gizmo's don't sell. Duh! So, more attention is being paid on what features customers really want and need. Designers are finally listening and trying to make technology accessible, under-standable, and friendly.[2]

Maintaining a customer focus is difficult. Even the best companies sometimes stumble. There are classic examples where companies have tripped in their customer focus. The bigger the company the big-ger the stumble appears. Coke tinkered with its original formula and depressed sales forced the company to make a public apology as it went back to the original formula. IBM was criticized for being too at-tached to mainframe computers. General Motors was humbled when it produced full-sized expensive autos when the market clamored for smaller, high quality vehicles.

SCM MARKET DRIVEN STRATEGIES

Competitive supply chains are adaptive and harness the energy of bot-tom-up understanding of market opportunities, technological abilities, team synergies, customer closeness, and top-down leadership, vision, and direction.[3]

There are a number of excellent strategic supply chain models. We have found the ones that focus on customer requirements work best. The common denominator of most of these strategies is fanatical cus-tomer and market focus. In **Market Driven Strategies**, George Day outlined the following simple framework of a customer-focused strategy.

- **Arena.** The arena component consists of the markets that a company and its supply chain want to target and serve. The arena identifies the customers to be served and the critical suc-cess factors needed to satisfy these customers.

- **Advantage.** Someone said that competitive advantage isn't be-tween companies but between supply chains. The advantage component consists of the supply chain competencies that dif-ferentiate a company and its supply chain from its competition. The competencies are the competitive advantages that a com-pany has to attract specific customers.

- **Access.** The access component is the supply chain technology, distribution and communication channels that are used to reach customers. Marketing channels, specialized niches, supply processes, logistics, and distribution strengths are the means to access specific customers.

- **Activities.** The activities component is what a company must do to transform supply chain inputs into what a customer wants, values, and purchases.

MASS CUSTOMIZATION

FISH: First in. Still Here.
Anonymous

Customers want greater product selectivity at a reduced cost, while having it easily accessible. How is done? Mass customization is today's preferred method, which basically says that a product will be tailored to the needs of the individual customer.

WHAT IS MASS CUSTOMIZATION?

Mass customization is a marketing philosophy that is a major driver of supply chain management. Mass customization implies that by using a standard product, different customers can be provided with specialized products. Specific customer features, work/feel, functionality, and bells/whistles can be added to the basic product to satisfy different customer segments and requirements.

The challenge is that mass customization requires supply chain flexibility. Manufacturers may have to build 20 or more different products using the same production line one week and 10 or more different products on the same line the following week or next day.

THE $5 TOOTHBRUSH

In the hyperactive toothbrush market, manufacturers are mass customizing by adding features for different users based on a common brush

---

CONTEXT: Dell Build to Order (BTO)

Dell is often cited as the poster company with the best BTO processes. Their BTO business model works this way:

A customer orders a computer directly by phone or by email. The customer only has a few computer options and features. The customer pays upfront by credit card. The computer is then assembled and sent within 3 days of the order.

The secret to Dell's BTO is to design standardized systems and modules that can be configured and assembled quickly. Dell suppliers provide preassembled systems and modules on demand. Dell restricts customer choice to a few modules and options that can be assembled within 4 minutes of the customer order. Installing the software takes about 90 minutes longer. Most of the customer customization comes from the software that is chosen by the customer.

By leaving customization to the end of production, Dell is able to mass-produce computers while leaving the 'customer of one' customization to the end of the buy process.[4]

---

platform. They design bristles of varying lengths, add new materials, and provide flexible handles. And instead of focusing on cavity prevention, the new brushes allegedly lower gum disease.

Would you pay $5 for a new premium toothbrush, which is basically a disposable, commodity product? Oral-B Laboratories bet you would. It's the most expensive mass-market toothbrush ever. What's different about it? It offers a number of critical innovative, customer value attributes. It has three types of multi-colored bristles set at different angles. The dense tip cleans behind back teeth. The handle is rubberized and ergonomically designed. It looks and feels cool. And, it sells for 50% more than its traditional high-end rivals.[5]

CONTEXT: VW Mass Customization

What is happening in VW is a common example of auto industry mass customization. VW shrank the number of automobile components among its brands, for example cutting the number of vehicle platforms from 16 to 4.

Eight separate cars with four marques will be based on VW's workhorse Golf platform. Customers are not stupid so mass customization must be carried out carefully. Customers may wonder why pay more for VW's premier Audi brands, when they can get pretty much the same technology more cheaply in a VW. "The trick ... is to make cars that are identical in ways that customers can't see and distinctive in ways that customers notice."[6]

What's happening? Motivating customers to trade up to a new generation of products through mass-customization in a seemingly mundane product can be a highly profitable strategy. A company can get both high volume and high profit margins simultaneously. Companies may develop a new product or jazz up a consumer product and charge a premium for them. Nike did it with its $150 sneakers. Starbucks did it with its $3 to $4 exotic coffee blends. Gillette did it with its Mach 3 razor.

SUPPLY CHAIN CHALLENGES TO MASS CUSTOMIZATION

To mass customize, four supply chain challenges must be addressed:

- **Smaller lot sizes.** Reducing process 'change over' and machine 'set up exchange' times become critical to producing different products in different lot quantities.

- **Information requirements increase exponentially with the number of suppliers and products.** As the number of products increases, the variation of product attributes, costs, delivery information and so on increases to the point where sophisticated computerized networks are required to monitor throughput, plan/forecast demand, store information, and anticipate supply chain bottlenecks.

- **Short production cycles make it difficult to fine tune production processes, much less supply chain processes.** Supply chain process and product spikes create supply chain bottlenecks, constraints, exceptions, and nonconformances.

- **Business relationships in the supply chain become much more complex.** Traditionally, customer-supply relationships were transaction or product based. Now, they are process based, incorporating process competencies of the supply chain partners.[7]

CUSTOMER VALUE ATTRIBUTES

Always define your terms.
Eric Partridge

A challenge and priority among supply chain partners is to identify key customer value attributes, develop appropriate customer satisfaction measures, and identify supply chain partners to provide these in an integrated fashion.

PRODUCT/SERVICE VALUE ATTRIBUTES

A company will determine what product/service value attributes matter to the customer and then determine which can or should be made in-house. Once this strategic decision is made, the company will outsource design, production, delivery, and product service to key supply-partners.

Supply management is responsible for managing these outsourced activities. Customer requirements are categorized into product value attributes or service value dimensions. Some value attributes are measurable and some are imprecise. For example, a value attribute, like aesthetics, may not be directly measurable. On the other hand, product performance is probably measurable.

Supply management will then require supply-partners to develop stable and capable design, production, delivery, and service processes. The goal is to create product consistency, specifically through defining, controlling, and continuously measuring the critical process and product attributes that matter to the customer.

VALUE DIMENSIONS

David Garvin, a Harvard Business School professor, recognized the problem of multiple definitions and identified nine quality categories, which we have extended to the following value dimensions.

- Performance.

- Reliability.

- Conformance.

- Usability.

- Maintainability.

- Customer service.

- Aesthetics.

- Environmental.

- Software quality.[8]

These value attributes are important because they define what a customer wants and define how the attribute will be delivered to the customer. In the following discussion, you will notice there are two elements: 1. the value attribute and 2. a measure of the value attribute. Both of which must be communicated to critical supply chain stakeholders, especially supply-partners. The ability to consistently deliver these value attributes to customers is what drives the supply value chain.

Performance

Performance is the ability of a product to operate up to the expectations of the user. Performance is measured differently in different products. In an automobile, performance includes acceleration, braking, and handling ability. And in a pair of running shoes, it includes comfort, style, durability, and weight.

Performance is a user-based definition of value, which means that an automobile can satisfy different expectations of different users. For example, a racecar driver expects a different level of performance from an Indy Ford compared to a Ford Focus.

Suppliers also are expected to improve a product's performance, packaging, reliability, and maintainability. Improvement may vary based on the type of product, such as whether it's an industrial or consumer product. Let us look at a computer. Making it operate faster and transmit more information may enhance the performance of a personal computer. Packaging can be improved by making it more aesthetic, easier to operate (user friendly), lightweight, and more compact.

Reliability

Reliability is long-term quality and is the probability of a product failing after a specified period of time under certain operating conditions. In other words, reliability measures the likelihood that a product or assembly will work over time. Reliability is both a user-based and a conformance-based, value attribute. For example, if a customer buys a lamp with a one-year warranty, the customer expects it to last at least one year. Otherwise, the customer will return it for repair, refund, or replacement. The lamp manufacturer knows this and does not want to spend much money replacing defective lamps. Therefore, the lamp is designed and manufactured to last at least one year.

Reliability is measured in terms of mean-time-between-failure (MTBF) or mean-time-to-first failure (MTFF). MTBF is the average time it takes a product to fail between two successive failures. MTFF is the average time it takes a product to fail based on the first time it's put into service.

CONTEXT: 7 Deadly Sins

- Inconsistent product quality (value).
- Slow response to the marketplace.
- Lack of innovative, competitive products.
- Uncompetitive cost structure.
- Inadequate employee involvement.
- Unresponsive customer service.
- Inefficient resource allocation.[9]

For example, automobile manufacturers know what parts of an automobile will likely fail, so they suggest checking and replacing parts based on a preventive maintenance schedule.

Conformance

Conformance is the ability of a product to comply with a specification, standard, or design. There are thousands of standards that specify how a product should be designed, built, tested, installed, stored, maintained, and repaired. For example, a screw is a simple fastener that holds one part onto another. A screw specification may designate height, width, thread taper, threads per inch, material, and material strength.

Conformance is an engineering or manufacturing definition of product value, because it's related to a feature of a product that can be measured. Conformance is measured in terms of defects rates or levels. For example, a specification for a screw may state that a certain type of screw should have 11 threads per inch and should be made of soft steel. If a screw randomly selected and inspected from a lot has 12 threads per inch and is made of stainless steel, then the screw has two nonconformances. These are defects, even though the screw has more threads per inch and is made of a stronger material than required by the specification.

CONTEXT: Ford Auto Company

User friendliness is a critical design feature of even the simplest but most important product. Ford Motor Company redesigned its Taurus and Sable. In the previous model, customers had complained that dashboard instrumentation had too many buttons, switches, and gages. The buttons were either too small, too large, too close together, or too difficult to read. This could also be dangerous if a busy instrumentation cluster distracted the driver.

So, Ford engineers redesigned the cluster to make it easier to read and use. Specifically, the controls became readily identifiable, easily accessible, aesthetically pleasing, and reflected the oval design of the vehicle.[11]

Usability

Usability is a key product attribute. A product may have all the technical bells and whistles, but it should be user friendly. All of us have been frustrated in trying to use software that simply does not work. The reasons may be technical incompatibility, poor documentation, user inability, or a number other reasons. One company that has tested hundreds of software products uncovered many blunders, including excessive technical jargon, overuse of icons, over reliance on training to overcome poor software design, cryptic error messages, and poorly conceived help systems.[10]

Maintainability

Maintainability is the same as serviceability. It's the ability of a defective product to be repaired easily, quickly, and economically. For example if an automotive water pump fails, it has to be replaced. But first, the automotive equipment in the way of the water pump has to be removed. Since the compact car was designed to be light weight, the area under the hood is tight and everything is squeezed into a small space. This decreases automobile weight and also decreases serviceability because the automobile is harder to work on.

This value attribute is both a conformance- and user- based definition. In an engineering sense, maintainability can be measured. A common measurement is mean-time-to-repair (MTTR), which is the average time it takes to repair a defective water pump or service a customer. In a user-based sense, maintainability reflects how the customer feels about replacing the defective unit. Was it easy to replace? Did the person get bruised knuckles? Could it be done quickly? Or, if a serviceman at a repair station performed the work, was the service courteous, fast, and economical?

Customer Service
Customer service is an important value attribute used to encourage re-peat sales. So, companies design products that can be serviced easily and safely. And companies are providing faster turnaround service to repair defective products. For example, Caterpillar Tractor promises it will deliver repair parts anywhere in the world within 48 hours and Mer-cedes guarantees 24-hour service in California and Arizona.[12]

Aesthetics
Aesthetics consist of the intangible value attributes: how a product looks, feels, sounds, tastes, or smells. Obviously, aesthetics are sub-jective, but they are a very important user-based attribute of brand value.

Many people buy a car not based on measurable, technical features of conformance or reliability, but on their value perceptions of quality, fit, and finish of the vehicle. People are often more concerned about the 'fit and finish' of an automobile than the technology inside, such as a new turbocharger. Or, they buy based on current and faddish styling standards. The same can be said for a number of other major consumer purchases, such as in apparel and fashion industries.

Environmental
Environmental groups and regulatory authorities are important stake-holders in the supply chain process. Many perceive that resources are

CONTEXT: The Common Tire

All organizations are scrambling to improve product performance and to minimize risks, such as with the common tire. The tire market is a global and mature market with many competitors. Tire makers use technology to differentiate themselves and minimize risks from a crowded market. It's a product we all use and are familiar with. Tire makers, such as Michelin, use children to communicate product value, such as safety. TV ads show sport utility vehicles navigating treacherous terrain in specialty tires. Tire makers demonstrate and promote their technical attributes, such as Goodyear's ads demonstrate how Aquatreds plow through water.[13]

being used and abused. The world's environment is radically changing as indicated through the ozone depletion, unbreathable air in American cities, toxic waste sites, and the list goes on. Sustainability is now the rallying cry of many concerned organizations that are listening to green consumers.

Businesses are now listening as a result of the Valdez oil spill, Three Mile Island, and other environmental disasters. Environmental concerns go well beyond being better corporate citizens, companies want to improve their public-customer perceptions, limit their legal exposure, and manage resources through recycling. Compliance to regulations is moving toward lean management of resources. How is this done? Companies are designing highly reliable and maintainable products. Packaging uses recycled materials. Obsolete products are recycled or disposed cleanly.

Software Quality
Software is integral to all products. In a few years, we are going to have 'smart' toasters and washing machines. Software value, just like any tangible product, must satisfy users requirements, comply with relevant standards, be cost-effective, and be measurable. For example, software must also be interoperable, intraoperable and exhibit a number of other value characteristics.

'MAKE OR BUY' DECISION

Any business must always plan ahead, either to capitalize on success or to reverse the trend if not successful.
Anonymous

Once a company has identified its customer value attributes, it must decide if it has the internal capabilities and resources to satisfy these customer requirements. The strategic question is: 'should we make or buy these products/services.' The 'make' decision is to bring the product in-house and produce it. The 'buy' decision is to purchase or source it.

'MAKE OR BUY'

The 'make or buy' decision is one of the most critical supply chain, strategic decisions. The supply management organization has à key role in this decision. The decision is important for a number of reasons. It determines and defines an organization's core competencies. It determines what level of investment the business should make internally as well as with suppliers.

The 'make or buy' decision involves financial and capability issues as companies ask: 'Do we have the expertise to manufacture a quality product and deliver it at a competitive cost?' Since some industrial tasks cannot be effectively accomplished in-house because of lack of equipment, trained personnel, or material, the answer to the question is often 'no.' So, non-core products and services are contracted to outside suppliers.

High Tech Companies

Let us look at a high-tech company's 'make or buy' decision-making. Following the rule, 'can't be all things to all customers,' high tech companies focus their internal resources on some core technology while depending on strategically outsourced innovations to complement their efforts.[14] In general, high tech companies such as Intel and Microsoft competitively position themselves based on their core knowledge competencies so that internal development ('make' decision) provides the

---

CONTEXT: Customer Focused Technology

Technology in all products focuses on making the customer's life and work simpler. Let us look at Chrysler's Jeep Cherokee. Its climate control system uses infrared beams to track driver's and passenger's skin temperature, adjusting the heat and air conditioning to keep passengers comfortable in the snow and desert. Even the trip display speaks five languages. [15]

---

most competitive advantage. In areas away from chip design and software development, they may outsource, license, or purchase required competencies.

'MAKE OR BUY' DUE DILIGENCE

If a company sources a product or service, then it can work with existing suppliers or find new suppliers. As much as possible, companies don't want surprises or variability. They want consistency. They want to work with known people, known relationships, and known processes. It's pretty simple; life and business work better when we work with knowns. Again, think variability. We don't want unknown variability, unknown risk, unknown people, unknown processes, or unknown suppliers.

The solution is to encourage supply-partnering relationships. Customers and suppliers must trust each other to share key process information, technologies, cost/delivery/quality targets, and even investments. This frankly isn't easy. It requires trust that a nondisclosure agreement can't enforce.

The 'make' decision also isn't easy for a supplier. The supplier may even pass on the opportunity to provide the product or service. The products may not be worthwhile to manufacture. The products may be low volume or 'one of a kind' that may require new production equipment or provide insufficient margins. Is the customer willing to pay for the added supplier investment? Many questions - few easy answers. The 'make or buy' decision usually comes down to optimizing many factors

ALTERNATE SOURCING OPTIONS

Also, the 'make or buy' decision involves a 'risk/reward' or 'cost/benefit' analysis. For example, low value products are usually commodity and non-strategic items. As well, there are multiple suppliers who can produce this commodity so the risk of losing a commodity source or finding competitive bidders is relatively low. If the supplier provides a high value, innovative product or process technology, the company may partner with a supplier or bring the product in-house.

What does a company do if a new or existent supplier can't produce the product to the customer's requirements? The customer has several options. It can find a new supplier or it can work with an existing supplier. The customer may even improve the supplier's capabilities. How? The customer can provide technical assistance, machines, incentives, or even pay the cost of improving the supplier's capabilities.

And, there is the 'risk-reward' decision of switching suppliers. This isn't negligible. The risk or cost of an unknown supplier may be too high. When should a company change a supplier? The change should occur when the cost, pain or risk of keeping the supplier exceed the cost of finding a new supplier.

All of these strategies work. The decision depends on the 'risk-reward' profile of the product or service supplier. Usually, the higher the product value, the higher the risk, the higher the required assurance and controls the customer wants, the higher the chance it will in-source the product or service.

SUMMARY

Customer satisfaction will drive all business decisions. The *Economist Magazine* concluded the following:

> "Already, many companies find it more of a struggle than they did to win new customers and to keep those they already have. No surprise there: competition has sprung up from all sorts of new directions in the past few frenetic years and it will intensify

---

CONTEXT: 'Make or Buy' Critical Questions

- What are your technology and information core competencies?
- Do you have internal processes to make it cheaper, better, etc. than others?
- Who is your competition?
- What are their core competencies?
- Do your suppliers have core competencies that complement yours?
- Which suppliers have competencies to make and deliver the product or service effectively, efficiently, and economically?
- What are the risks and benefits of insourcing (make it), outsourcing to existing suppliers (buy it) and outsourcing to new suppliers (buy it)?

---

as the downturn makes customers both pickier and more cautious."[16]

Supply chain management matters to everyone from the CEO to the person on the line. Without a reliable flow of supplied products and services, there are no products to deliver on time, on budget to satisfied customers. Some supply chain pundits now say that sourcing efficiencies have the greatest potential to impact the bottom line.

If you're involved with supply chain issues, this is your time. Many buying, logistics, and materials people have been in lower level, operational and management positions. Supply management is now a competitive strategic issue. This is a great time to make a difference in your career and to your company.

As a matter of fact, strategic sourcing and supply chain management have attained such high-level corporate visibility, that more people are moving from finance, operations, engineering, and information technology to supply management.

CHAPTER 5:
SUPPLY CHAIN STRATEGIES

Jack Welch, former CEO of General Electric, popularized the concept of the boundaryless organization where artificial boundaries to resources, communication and cooperation are removed to improve business processes. Technology and instant communication facilitate the redesign of organizational processes through the removal of horizontal barriers within the organization, the vertical barriers in the organizational hierarchy, and the external barriers outside a department or business unit or in other words throughout the supply chain.

WHEN CHANGE HAPPENS!
Leadership appears to be the art of getting others to want to do something you are convinced should be done.
Vance Packard

How does a company become competitive and adopt supply chain management?   This is a critical question to all supply management organizations. Companies are investing in improvement activities when the need isn't fully understood or articulated.

WHAT DRIVES THE NEED FOR SCM?
The following are early warning signs that SCM change – evolutionary or transformational - may be necessary:

- Changing competitive environment.

- Low internal and external customer satisfaction.

- Few or no performance measures.

- Slow or very fast company growth.

- Mergers, acquisitions, reengineering, or other transformations.

- Competitive loss.

- Inflexible or fat supply chain.

- No senior management SCM commitment.

- Strong departmental silos.

- Low profit margins.

- Poor intra and inter customer-supply communications.

- More supply chain talks and planning than action.

- Ineffective suppliers.

- Unclear supply chain goals.

- No emphasis on supply management training or learning.

- Resistance to change.

INCREASING RATE OF CHANGE

Something and someone have to be the impetus and catalyst for supply management change like a new competitor, increasing/changing customer expectations, regulatory oversight, product liability litigation, or a monumental supply event. External SCM drivers to an organizational change or transformation can involve losing market share, product recalls, pending litigation, regulatory action, new regulations, negative customer surveys, or mounting losses. The event says the ways of doing things are no longer acceptable and things must be done differently.

As the velocity, the rate of change, of technology increases; organizations must adapt and anticipate these changes. Supply chain management is often a favored approach. The problem is the purpose of an organization and its supply base is challenged. Companies, organizations, and institutions have a body of culture, values, principles, and infrastructure that seems to value the status quo in direct challenge to the acceleration of technology and the need for competitiveness.

THE BEST COMPANIES LOVE CHANGE

The best companies have a culture that thrives on change - technology, customer, system, competitor, and marketplace changes. The faster the rate of change, the more these organizations thrive. Cycle times are reduced. New value added technologies are rapidly deployed. These companies use change to maintain their competitive edge and to enhance profitability. It isn't a matter of being left behind but of anticipating customer expectations and leapfrogging the competition.

How is this done? The best companies quickly develop, test, and tweak new technologies, core processes, and organizational structures to be flexible and competitive. This is what is being done with SCM. Supply managers are encouraged and rewarded to learn, adapt, and adopt new technologies. The best supply management processes are built to encourage flexibility, quickness, and compatibility. Products are developed quickly. Virtual supply-partners are selected. A culture of rapid innovation and lean improvement is emphasized daily. The organizational challenge is that promoters of the status-quo can suffer in this environment.

INCREMENTAL VS. TRANSFORMATIONAL CHANGE

A competitive world has two possibilities for you. You can lose. Or, if you want to win, you can change.
Lester Thurow, Management Professor

There was an ad for Putnam Investments: "You think you understand the situation, but what you don't understand is that the situation just changed." Amen! When I think I've got it, 'got' and 'it' both changed. It's scary and at the same time exciting – the thrill of being in supply management when the rules seem to change overnight.

Supply chain management is a process change paradigm. Competitiveness is the driver for companies to 'focus on what they do well' and SCM is the means by which companies can secure reliable suppliers that also 'focus on what they do well.'

SUPPLY MANAGEMENT IS CHANGE MANAGEMENT

All supply management activities can be distilled into one premise: change management. The best-designed and well-intentioned supply chain initiatives will fail to deliver business performance unless the organizational and human dimensions of implementation are adequately addressed. Any organizational change, incremental or transformational, is immensely difficult to accomplish. Supply chain executives must create change-ready organizations.

Some organizations are more conducive to change than others. Mature companies in commodity or regulated industries are less likely to change because of entrenched practices, top-heavy hierarchies, and inflexible cultures. Continuous improvement and innovation tend to flourish in companies and industries where the marketplace requires speed and flexibility. Supply chain systems and processes by necessity must be flexible to adapt to a dynamic marketplace where customers want 'built to order' products. Supply chain processes must be lean, congruent, supportive, and reinforce the culture of key supply partners.

DIFFERENCE BETWEEN INCREMENTAL CHANGE AND TRANSFORMATION

Organizational change and transformation processes are fundamentally different. According to Richard Pascale, author of **Managing on the Edge**, change is 'incremental improvement' while transformation is a 'discontinuous shift in capability.' He defines transformation as a discontinuous shift in bottom line results, industry standards, benchmarks, and employee perceptions. From this definition, supply chains can be seen as a discontinuous shift from prior purchasing or sourcing practices.

The transformation process results in major supply chain changes that are brought about by engaged stakeholders. These stakeholders view transformed customer-supply relationships and expectations as a different business model from that of 2 years ago. While incremental change is sufficient for many well performing companies, a supply chain stakeholder in a highly competitive market segment may have to transform continuously.[1]

MANAGING CHANGE

Managing supply change is a difficult process. The process has to respect supplier rights, comply with regulations, comply with work agreements, be ethical, and in the end be effective. Supply chain change becomes more difficult as international boundaries, financial exigencies, political constraints, cultural pressures, and other factors increase.

Change and transformation may involve a certain amount of organizational, management, supplier, and individual discomfort. The challenge is to institutionalize discomfort so it becomes part of the supply chain fabric, ethic, and culture. In other words, marketplace pressures and customer requirements are communicated throughout the supply chain so stakeholders become flexible and almost anticipate the need for change.

This is difficult because extreme, external pressures can stymie initiative. Organizations become frozen through fear of downsizing. Suppliers become frozen through fear of being eliminated. The supply chain may be redesigned. Suppliers are integrated into the product development process.

Resistance is normal and expected when the supply chain is formed and organizations must change. Resistance may occur initially, disappear, or continue throughout the supply change process. What is the supply change agent or team supposed to do with pockets of resistance? Most supply chain stakeholders are rational and will understand the need for change if it's plainly explained and if the urgency is particularly evident. Change may also be induced through financial incentives, training, promotion, or other mechanisms.

LEADING THE CHANGE

A fundamental challenge to all executives, including the chief supply executive, is managing change. For some managers, this involves being proactive, embracing change, searching for new opportunities and capitalizing on them. For others, this means surviving the latest management fad or simply maintaining purchasing head count in a downsizing workplace.

The chief supply chain executive is often called the chief purchasing officer (CPO). This person should lead the supply change initiative. The transformation can't be delegated. The CPO must make it a top priority otherwise it won't happen.

The essential element behind any supply chain transformation is a person or team that catalyses the transformation. Often, the CPO works with a core group of senior executives to deploy the SCM initiative. If senior management and the board of directors make the transformation a priority, devote time, assign resources, and manage it then it has a much higher chance of success.

There is a direct correlation between the level of project sponsorship and project success. A study by the Warehouse and Research Council and Andersen Consulting revealed that only 7% of supply chain projects were rated as 'very successful' - all were sponsored by a VP or higher manager. [2]

Successful SCM transformations require:

- Customer driven supply chain orientation.
- Sense of competitive urgency.

CONTEXT: Supply Change Agent Responsibilities

- Provide a roadmap to change.
- Facilitate meetings.
- Provide training and role model team leaders.
- Analyze supply problems and offer solutions.
- Intervene at critical junctures.
- Resolve supply chain conflicts.
- Provide objective and independent evaluations of the process.
- Provide suggestions for supply chain improvement.

THE TRANSFORMATION PROCESS

The supply chain transformation first starts internally by 1. establishing supply chain drivers and 2. eliminating supply chain inhibitors. Supply chain transformation drivers include senior management commitment, customer satisfaction, and competitive focus. Supply chain inhibitors are any elements that obstruct the supply chain initiative. Inhibitors may include departmental resistance, internal functional boundaries, supplier fears, politics, and other forms of resistance.

If senior management feels comfortable with command and control, the driver approach can be used internally. Senior management first will establish the SCM mandate for change and then start integrating various SCM elements including supply development, six sigma, ERP, MRP, lean or ISO 9001:2015 registration throughout the organization and then into the supply stream.

This isn't an easy process. Driving a supply partnering or six-sigma process can cause additional organizational stress and strain. It's more effective to use a combination of drivers and inducements to shape or direct change.

Freeing the organization from existing ways of doing things is difficult but is recognized as an effective means for inducing change. In general, it's wiser to proceed slowly, show daily commitment to the change

> **CONTEXT: Rules for Leading the SCM Transformation**
>
> - Develop and follow a strategic supply chain vision.
> - Clarify core competencies and values.
> - Conduct supply chain and organizational readiness assessment.
> - Get suppliers and other supply chain members involved.
> - Lead and inspire the initiative.
> - Communicate.
> - Have a bottom line, financial focus.
> - Provide supply management and stakeholder training.
> - Establish a personal recognition program.
> - Sense of business and supply chain alignment.
> - Active CPO and senior management involvement.
> - Long term supply management view and mandate.
> - Involvement and acceptance by all organizational stakeholders.
> - Extensive individual training and development.
> - Extensive supply development.

process, understand actions speak louder than words, couple supply security with empowerment, and reinforce actions that support the SCM initiative.

INFLUENCING THE SUPPLY CHAIN

Unfortunately, consequencers and negative reinforcers seem to be the common means for forcing supply change. Supply base reduction is now a fact of business life and may be an integral element of the SCM initiative. This creates new and worrisome challenges for the supply manager and suppliers as they try to figure out new customer-supply rules. Supply management priorities become unclear during such times. Everyone is looking for cost cutting opportunities, which may conflict with the overall customer-supply partnering messages and opportunities.

What is the role of the supply chain professional in these turbulent times especially if he or she is the change agent? The role of the supply change agent is difficult in the best of times and is very difficult in these downsizing times. In change resistant organizations, the supply manager may feel she or he has a bulls-eye on her back. Why? Change may be transformational instead of evolutionary. Senior management may not totally understand and support the supply chain initiative. There may be pockets of resistance. The organization isn't adaptable or people don't have the skills to affect change. Cynicism becomes widespread over the newest fad. People already are too busy on day-to-day operations and don't have time for the new supply chain project or methodology. The wrong person may have been chosen to lead the supply change initiative. Whatever the cause, the result is the same. The supply chain transformation and initiative tend to bog down and get sidetracked. Key people including supply management professionals become discouraged over the floundering initiative.

SCM MISSION LINKS WITH BUSINESS STRATEGIES

Success is that old ABC - ability, breaks, and courage.
Charles Luckman, architect

A strategic plan focuses on where the organization intends to go. A company may want to enter new markets, develop new products, or offer new services. Each activity from conception to delivery has a number of supply chain components. The job of supply management is to identify supply components that touch on the overall strategy and develop tactics that align, support and enhance the overall business model.

FROM TACTICAL TO STRATEGIC

James Morgan, the editor of *Sourcing,* said the following about the evolution from a tactical to a strategic purchasing perspective:

> "Perhaps the most encouraging and daunting demand from top management is the strategies hot button. Until very recently, top management often treated supply/sourcing as a sort of semi-function. It was the center of much activity, but had little linkage to the corporate operating plan."

> **CONTEXT: Pursue Value First**
>
> "Strategy starts with an overall understanding of the opportunity for value," said William S. Schaefer, VP of IBM Procurement Services in an ISM workshop.[4] From this value perspective, IBM developed the following strategic imperatives:
>
> - Continually deliver the lowest overall cost and greatest competitive value.
> - Establish premiere supplier relationships.
> - Attain e-procurement leadership.
> - Continually drive improved client perceptions of value through increased influence and exemplary customer service.
> - Attract, motivate, and retain the best talent within our profession.[5]

"This year's survey seems to trace a highly significant change in perspective on the part of many senior managers. Where in the past, purchasers were at best considered as implementers of supply strategy, a growing segment of executive management appears to be looking for a degree of buying/sourcing/supply strategizing on the part of the sourcing organization. But while top management appears to be inclined to bestow greater responsibilities to sourcing organizations, it still isn't clear what the responsibility boundaries will look like. In other words, sourcing hasn't won complete authority over sourcing and supply - just a measure of responsibility for its direction."[3]

STRATEGIC ALIGNMENT

The supply management professional must align all supply processes, relationships, and contracts with the organization's strategic plan. The supply manager does this by reinforcing organizational values, empowering customer-supply teams, satisfying internal customers, cutting costs, facilitating inter/intra departmental relations, and improving overall supply management efficiencies. For example, senior management will never criticize aligned initiatives that support customers or improve the organization in cost-effective ways.

A critical way to support and reinforce supply chain strategic alignment is through developing trust and commitment among operating managers. Operational management support is critical because they have the authority, responsibility and resources to get supply management projects started and finished.

SCM STRATEGIZING

Leadership is the act of taking people somewhere with an idea - visioning them into the future and then taking them there.
Richard S. Johnson

A vision is a "realistic, credible, attractive future for your organization."[6] The vision is a statement of where the organization, supply chain, plant, department, team or even individual wants to be in the future. The vision statement provides a destination the organization and supply chain can aim towards. A vision deals with future, probable outcomes. The vision should be energizing. It should be easy to understand and easy to identify with. The vision should jump-start an organization and supply chain to focus on what needs to be done and can be done.

LINK SUPPLY MANAGEMENT WITH THE STRATEGIC VISION

The above quote by Richard S. Johnson sums up the supply chain visioning process. The vision process starts with supply chain stakeholders articulating and then distilling a supply direction for the organization and inducing critical supply-partners in this direction. The supply chain vision is then an ongoing, never ending statement that is continually updated depending on marketplace requirements and supply chain opportunities. The transformational leader or CPO uses the vision to help define where the supply chain is and where it can be in the future.

Strategic SCM planning and thinking form the basis of what the supply chain will look like and what markets it will serve years down the road. A well crafted supply chain vision establishes an attainable benchmark, defines a path, energizes and encourages, provides meaning to supply owners, is simple and readily understood, and creates a sense of urgency. Examples of common vision statements include the U.S. Constitution, Kennedy's 'we shall put a man on the moon' speech and Ford Motor's Company 'Quality is Job 1.' One company's vision was 'putting the value in the value chain.' Or, one supply manager recently told me their unwritten supply chain vision is: 'our supply chain can beat yours' (the competitors).

SUPPLY CHAIN VISIONING

The supply chain vision requires strong leadership, knowledge of organizational dynamics, sensitivity of supply chain politics, understanding of the competitive marketplace and desire to satisfy customer expectations. Once the supply chain vision is developed, supply managers can develop and deploy goals, plans, and objectives. The supply management vision is then supported through words and deeds by senior management.

Supply chain visioning process should encourage stakeholders to burst out of self-imposed barriers, to think 'outside the purchasing box.' Specific issues to consider are:

- **Scope of the supply management vision.** The vision should be tailored to the purpose, competencies and scope of the supply base. The vision statement for a corporate supply management function, business unit, plant or supply team would be different.

- **Vision of the organization.** The supply management vision and mission statements should link, echo, and reinforce the organizational strategic vision.

- **Culture of the organization.** The supply management vision should dovetail with the organizational culture. For example, a supply management vision emphasizing Darwinist competitiveness may be inappropriate in an organization that fosters customer-supply collaboration and partnering.

- **Core competencies.** The core competencies of the supply management organization should be understood, articulated, and emphasized in the vision and mission statements. Core competencies allow the supply management organization to achieve its vision.

- **Resources.** Resources should be dedicated and available for achieving the vision.

SUPPLY CHAIN MISSION STATEMENT

While similar, a vision and a mission statement are often different. A vision defines the supply chain direction. A supply chain mission defines its purpose, its reason for existing. The mission statement may define, for example, what the supply organization has been established to do, such as integrate 'world class' suppliers into a seamless chain.

The mission statement clarifies supply management vision, direction, and goals thereby allowing employees and other stakeholders to understand their roles in ensuring success. The mission statement also provides a reference point from which supply management plans and objectives can be measured, monitored, and assessed.

A vision or mission statement may be short or can be all encompassing. I prefer short statements that distill the purpose of the organization such as Daimler Chrysler's purpose is to 'produce cars and trucks that people will want to buy, will enjoy driving, and will want to buy again' or Microsoft's vision is to put 'a computer on every desk and in every home.'

SCM PLANNING

Planning is the process by which profitable growth is sought and attained in a changing and uncertain world.
Anonymous

As one climbs the supply management hierarchy, planning becomes more critical and time consuming. The Chief Purchasing Officer will spend much of his or her time planning strategy and developing suppliers. Why? Poor planning is a major factor in the failure of supply improvement initiatives. Poor planning can create unrealistic expectations, poor understanding, and lack of direction.

James Morgan, a long time observer of purchasing changes, made the case for supply management planning:

> "To achieve competitive advantages through integrated supply chain management, businesses need to continue to emphasize their outsourcing strategies. Outsourcing can significantly benefit a firm if it's performed in the context of a strategic plan. Outsourcing adds little competitive benefit, however, to a firm that does not have a clear vision of its core competencies and knowledge of where it can compete versus what it should outsource."[7]

PURPOSE OF PLANNING

Many organizations still focus on product, tactical, or transactional supply planning emphasizing commodity forecasting, cost analysis, quality inspection, or product testing. While these are definitely important, the strategic supply chain issues dealing with customer satisfaction, supplier capabilities, make/buy decisions, supply development, and information systems sometimes are not addressed. Strategic business objectives that get management's immediate attention should be addressed in any supply management plan including revenue enhancement, cost reduction, innovative product development, and customer satisfaction improvement.

Supply chain planning basically is the process of selecting objectives and establishing a road map for meeting organizational objectives. Supply chain planning involves deciding where the SCM initiative should/can go, how to get there, who will lead it, what vehicles will be used, what are the milestones in the journey, and what are the expected outcomes upon arrival. The SCM road map may be a guideline document or a formal project document identifying customer requirements; prioritizing stakeholder requirements; developing a supplier list; defining cost/delivery/quality requirements; detailing supporting documentation; developing robust designs, bills of material, specifications; and so on.

WHY IS SCM PLANNING SO IMPORTANT?

Supply chain planning is critical because it:

- **Provides direction.** Supply chain planning provides direction for the organization to implement the supply chain initiative. Once an overall strategic direction is established, then more detailed tactical supply plans can be formulated for divisions, departments, teams, and product lines.

- **Provides a structured framework.** Planning provides a structured framework for supply chain decisions. Without a framework or plan, the supply chain initiative is rudderless and cannot achieve its goals. Each business unit or operational department may interpret a supply chain requirement differently, which affects implementation. A structured framework unifies different interpretations, goals, and tactics into a common effort that focuses on customer satisfaction.

- **Reveals opportunities.** Supply chain planning reveals opportunities to improve supply chain efficiencies, reduce costs, improve profits, increase market share, or please customers.

- **Facilitates supply control and assurance.** Contingency supply chain planning anticipates potential problems. Once areas of potential problems are uncovered, plans, corrective actions, and preventive actions can be developed to prevent their recurrence.[8]

STRATEGIC PLANNING

Strategic SCM plans have a two-year or longer horizon. They focus on the overall 'make/buy' decision, building internal capabilities, product/supplier risk analysis, contingency planning, demand schedules, and supply capability development.

Strategic SCM planning involves identifying customer wants, needs, and expectations regarding quality, delivery, technology, service, and cost factors and then developing sourcing capabilities to satisfy these expectations. Supply cost, technology, and logistics capabilities are especially critical success factors as customers want custom products developed and delivered quickly.

Strategic SCM plans explain how suppliers fit into the company's business mission. These plans ensure that senior management focuses on the long-term instead of short-term operational concerns. Senior management and the CPO then endorse and actively support these plans.

SUPPLY MANAGEMENT TACTICAL PLANS

Once strategic SCM plans are established, then yearly or quarterly SCM tactical plans are developed. Tactical plans detail how the SCM strategy will be deployed. Tactics are often step-by-step plans for action.

Tactical SCM plans are detailed, specific, and short term. Tactical plans may detail how a product is made or a service is delivered and detail how a product or service is sourced. In general, tactical supply management plans can specify what business areas or even product lines may be developed and how suppliers will be selected, developed, and improved.

CONTEXT: Strategic SCM Planning Elements

- Exceed customer expectations is the organizational mission.
- SCM is a core element of the organizational mission.
- Supplied products and services must please customers.
- Supplied products at a minimum must conform to standards and specifications.
- Specifications, standards, and procedures are realistic, attainable, and measurable.
- Lean supply processes are the means by which to attain business objectives.
- Real time process control and prevention are emphasized.
- Internal and supplier capability, quality, cost, delivery, and technology are continuously improved through supply development and integration.
- Suppliers are partners in the overall SCM system.

KEY PLANNING ELEMENTS

The following are key elements in all SCM planning:

- **Flexibility.** Any journey has switchbacks and dead ends. A SCM plan should be flexible so changes can be made easily.

- **Doability.** The plan should outline a workable and attainable route for the manufacturer as well as key supply-partners.

- **Realism.** The plan should be realistic given the internal and sourcing capabilities and resources.

- **Team based and driven.** The plan should incorporate the key stakeholders throughout the supply chain and throughout the product or contract lifecycle.

SCM DEPLOYMENT

Businesses aren't run by geniuses. It is a matter of putting one foot after another in a logical fashion. The trick is in knowing what direction you want to go.
James R. Barker

There is no one officially sanctioned or approved SCM deployment methodology. It seems that every consultant to differentiate himself or herself recommends something a little different. The following SCM methodology is a plain vanilla model that incorporates steps that seem to work:

- **Step 1**. Understand the competitive, business, and supply chain environment.

- **Step 2**. Establish supply chain environment.

- **Step 3**. Understand supply chain processes.

- **Step 4**. Identify performance improvement goals and objectives.

- **Step 5**. Establish supply chain organizational structure.

- **Step 6**. Implement supply chain improvement projects.

- **Step 7**. Evaluate project results and improvement.

- **Step 8**. Review and recycle (Go back to Step 1).[9]

STEP 1: UNDERSTAND THE COMPETITIVE, BUSINESS AND SUPPLY CHAIN ENVIRONMENT

A supply chain exists in a competitive, business and cultural environment. This must first be understood before SCM should be implemented. The purpose of this competitive analysis is to identify competitor's supply chains and gather information about the environment in which a supply chain competes. The playing field is between competing supply chains. This competitive analysis guides the development of SCM strategies and plans.

Competitive analysis is an ongoing process. As a company develops and implements SCM strategies, the results should be monitored on an ongoing basis to ensure the right things are being done on time. Continuous feedback monitoring allows for changes in make/buy decisions, supply development, and technology application.

A critical question in the competitive analysis is how to acquire core competencies. One method is through business acquisitions. Another is through supply chain alliances that reinforce internal core competencies and strengthen the business mix. If a company acquires a business or a supply-partner, it expects a synergistic effect of related businesses to reinforce the core systems.

Questions and factors to consider in a competitive SCM analysis include:

- What are the major economic, social, cultural, and technical trends impacting the business and supply chain over the next three years and one year?

- Who are the supply chain competitors?

- What are their relative strengths and weaknesses?

- Who may be tomorrow's supply chain competitors?

- In terms of today's competitors which point of weakness provides the greatest competitive leverage?

STEP 2: ESTABLISH SUPPLY CHAIN ENVIRONMENT

SCM is a total business, organizational, and technical approach towards developing internal and supplier systems, processes, and products that please customers. Senior management commitment and involvement are essential for SCM to flourish. Senior management takes the lead for creating a flexible SCM environment, defining the culture, and encouraging change.

Senior management is responsible for:

- Vision.

- Long term commitment.

- Active and visible support.

- People involvement and empowerment.

- Goals and objectives definition.

- Methodologies.

- Training.

- Organizational roadblock elimination.

Vision
Senior management and critical stakeholders establish a vision of supply chain possibilities. The visioning process links external market requirements, opportunities, and challenges to internal core process capabilities. If internal capabilities don't exist, they are developed internally or acquired from a supplier.

Long Term Commitment
SCM is a business process model and requires a long-term commitment to ensure its success. Customer requirements change over time and the SCM model also changes to accommodate today's customers as well as tomorrow's. For example a few years ago, purchasing was largely defined in terms of low price and ability to meet conformance requirements. Now, niche customers must be pleased with customized, cost competitive, aesthetically pleasing products and services that are delivered courteously and quickly.

Senior management commitment involves a number of visible activities, specifically providing:

- Long term supply chain perspective and drive.

- Focus on innovation, reengineering, and continuously improving business results.

- Policies defining the direction of the organization and supply chain.

- Supply chain standards specifying what is expected and accepted.

- Supply chain talks, speeches, and rewards.

- Monies, facilities, people, equipment, and other resources.

- Value added SCM training.

- Reward and recognition for satisfying and exceeding customer requirements.

People Involvement and Empowerment

People are the means of implementing SCM. Supply management professionals must own their processes. Senior management establishes, supports, and reinforces supply chain initiatives by rewarding stakeholders to submit ideas and to implement them within the supply chain without fear of reprisal.

SCM sometimes requires a change in how business is conducted if not an organizational and cultural transformation. It takes time and patience. The process may start with low-level supply participation and move toward more supply involvement, empowerment and finally customer-supply process integration.

The critical elements of success are faith, trust, and results. Faith is required to start the SCM process. Trust between the customer and supplier is required to ensure the process will proceed satisfactorily. Finally, demonstrable results ensure improved process capabilities.

Goals and Objectives
The goals and objectives of the SCM initiative must link, support, and reinforce the overall business vision, mission, plans, and objectives. These supplier linkages must be definable, demonstrable, timely, and measurable.

SCM initiatives were basically approved because they were viewed as good for the customer. Monies were allocated and spent with sometimes few results. Now, senior management and other stakeholders are smarter and regard SCM as an investment that must demonstrate immediate and sufficient financial return beyond the Business to Business (B2B) hype. Most importantly, these returns must support the critical business mission.

SCM Methodologies
SCM must follow a disciplined and integrated approach using the appropriate sourcing tools, methodologies, principles, and techniques. The right approach and tools must consider the culture of the supply chain organization. Supply management professionals must monitor the right supply chain control variables, recognized when there is an abnormality, intervene with the right tools, and remove the deficiency. This is called process management by exception, which is explained later in the book.

The following is a common SCM problem solving methodology:

- Analyze organizational, management, team, and individual issues.

- Analyze supplier systems, processes and products.

- Solve the supply problem.

- Stabilize and document the process.

- Ensure the supply process is capable.

- Improve the supply system and process.

- Audit the supply system for improvement.

Training

Changing customer requirements and new product development require continuous knowledge management and stakeholder training. New suppliers at a minimum are trained in how to integrate core capabilities with those of the customer's. Employees are trained in SCM tools, techniques, culture, customer requirements, processes, systems, and products.

STEP 3: UNDERSTAND SUPPLY CHAIN PROCESSES

The supply chain is a master process with a number of sub processes. To understand the supply chain and its various tributaries, the chain should be process mapped. Process mapping means that critical supply chain activities are flowcharted.

Depending on the supply chain's efficiency and effectiveness, it may have to be redesigned along integrated core process lines. Process redesign usually follows a 'gap analysis' of mapping the 'is' processes and developing a vision of the 'should be' supply chain processes. Process redesign moves the 'is' processes to the 'should be' supply chain processes. The speed by which this is done determines if the change is a transformation or an evolutionary change.

STEP 4: IDENTIFY PERFORMANCE IMPROVEMENT GOALS/OBJECTIVES

More often, supply chain improvement initiatives or projects are performance driven. Demonstrable results are tied to strategic business objectives. Improvement efforts are linked throughout the organization, across functional boundaries and into the supply stream.

The supply chain consists of a master process with a number of sub-processes. Critical process elements should have improvement goals

---

CONTEXT: Purchasing Inefficiencies

- Lack of customer requirement knowledge.
- Lack of internal core process knowledge.
- Lack of supply core process knowledge.
- Lack of customer and supplier core process integration knowledge.
- Authoritarian supply management.
- Transaction focused.
- Variations in specifications and contracts.
- Firefighting problem solving.
- Low cost focused.
- Lack of long term supplier relationships.
- Adversarial supply relationships.
- Multiple points of supplier contact.
- Limited knowledge of supply capabilities.
- Lack of supply base information.
- Lack of supply management talent.

---

and objectives. The chain is only as strong as its weakest link. As much as possible, the supply process chain should be standardized, documented, stabilized, capable, measured, and improved. Value adders are reinforced. Value reducers, such as waste, are eliminated. These can only be done if there are realistic measures.

Typical supply chain improvement projects or opportunities may involve:

- Improving supplier process capability.

- Improving product maintainability or reliability.

- Redesigning supply chain processes.

- Installing a new ERP or MRP module.

- Eliminating inventories.

- Lowering supply costs.

- Improving delivery and service.

- Improving customer satisfaction.

STEP 5: ESTABLISH SUPPLY CHAIN ORGANIZATIONAL STRUCTURE

SCM requires a coordinated structure to plan and deploy SCM projects, specifically:

- Corporate steering group.

- Business unit steering group.

- Supplier process improvement teams.

Corporate Steering Group

This senior level group focuses on the strategic direction of the SCM initiative. The Chief Purchasing Officer (CPO) often chairs this group. As well, this group:

- Establishes the vision.

- Develops guiding principles.

- Provides resources.

- Establishes internal and supplier rewards and recognition.

- Establishes metrics.

- Identifies process owners in business units.

Business Unit Steering Group

This operational management group focuses on the tactical direction of the supply management teams at the business unit or at the plant level. As well, this group:

- Analyzes internal systems and supplier processes.

- Identifies specific supply chain improvement opportunities.

- Establishes plans for achieving objectives and capitalizing on opportunities.

- Provides resources.

- Develops improvement plans.

- Measures and reports on progress.

- Provides operational coaching and mentoring.

- Develops supply management leaders and facilitators.

- Monitors internal and supplier processes for control and capability.

- Intervenes when required.

SCM Process Improvement Teams

These teams implement improvement project using established methodologies and techniques at the supply process and product level.

STEP 6: IMPLEMENT SUPPLY CHAIN IMPROVEMENT PROJECTS

The basic steps in a supply chain improvement project are:

- **Identify and prioritize supply chain improvement opportunities.** Opportunities can be identified and prioritized through Pareto analysis (80-20 rule) of the cost of quality, product lifecycle costs, return on investment, risk analysis, and force field analysis. SCM projects with the highest return, quickest return, or the highest risk are chosen and pursued first.

- **Flow chart (map) supply chain processes.** Before a supply improvement project is initiated, supply chain processes should be flowcharted. A supply flowchart shows the process chain as a series of steps or links. Each step has a customer and supplier. The flowchart can then be used to understand the supply process and to identify redundancies, waste, or other non-value added activities. The objective is to pursue lean initiatives. Specific techniques used to flowchart processes include: block diagrams, input/output analysis, benchmarking, and process redesign.

- **Assess fulfillment of final and internal customer needs.** Each process step has a customer whose needs must be satisfied. Customer satisfaction determines if the process is doing what it's supposed to be doing.

- **Develop and establish supply chain process measures.** The inputs, process, and outputs of the process can be measured. Measures may be customer, process or product specific. For example, process measures may look at speed, quality, cost, delivery, efficiency, or effectiveness.

- **Understand sources of supply process variation.** The measurement and control of variation is fundamental to all continuous improvement. Once data is collected and reviewed, then special causes of variation can be eliminated. Once the process is in control, then common or fundamental causes of variation can be identified and eliminated.

- **Control process variation.** Supply chain processes can then be controlled, standardized, and proceduralized. When a supply process has been stabilized, then it can be improved.

STEP 7: EVALUATE PROJECT RESULTS AND IMPROVEMENT

From a business perspective, measurement determines if SCM investments are worth it. Results may involve lowered costs, reduced deficiencies, reduced cycle times, improved productivity, improved customer satisfaction, or other specific factors.

Measurements may include:

- **Process measurements.** Process measures include external customer satisfaction, internal customer satisfaction, process control, and process capability.

- **Product measurements.** Product measurements include complying with dimensional, physical, or chemical specifications.

- **Project measurements.** Project measurements involve meeting budgets, completing the project on time, and complying with contractual requirements.

- **Product development measurements.** Product development measurements involve external customer satisfaction and cycle time reduction.

- **Behavioral/organizational measurements.** Behavioral measurements include improved quality of work life and increased work safety.

STEP 8: REVIEW AND RECYCLE[10]

One of W. Edwards Deming's (the quality guru) 14 points of quality management was 'constancy of purpose' which meant that process improvement was not instant pudding but required continuous attention and application. Supply chain management requires long-term commitment and effort from senior management and day-to-day commitment from each supply and organizational stakeholder.

Continuous supply chain improvement implies the process starts again when a project has been completed and a process has been stabilized. The improvement cycle may start with another supplier, expand to become a supply wide initiative or become a targeted supply improvement project.

CHANGE - READY SUPPLY MANAGERS

In the simplest terms, a leader is one who knows where she or he wants to go and gets up and goes.
John Erskine

Change initiatives fail unless there is a cultural fit. If there is a cultural interference fit, there is a high probability that any new initiative will fail, including supply chain management. Bottom line: strategic sourcing or supply chain management will succeed if the following exist: unity of purpose and shared wins/rewards among stakeholders.

CHANGING RULES

Transformations, by their nature, are not easy. An organization or supplier going through a transformation, not an incremental change, may experience a wrenching and abrupt process. Supply managers must live in a constantly changing and some would say, chaotic world. Why? The marketplace is global. Customer requirements are changing in the U.S. and throughout the world. Suppliers in developing nations are becoming formidable competitors with their own supply chains. There are no uniform rules.

FLATTER ORGANIZATIONS

Successful SCM requires that supply managers have the authority and responsibility to take risks and make intelligent decisions. Buyers are being elevated to supply managers with more decision-making authority.

Rigid, hierarchal, and authoritarian styles of purchasing management are becoming history. Supply managers are encouraged and rewarded to make decisions as part of a supply team. The supply management organization is more fluid, some say virtual, as supply teams are established to get a job done and are then disbanded. Command and control, first-line purchasing supervisors evolve into facilitators. Middle supply managers became coaches. Senior purchasing and supply managers become stewards and champions of the SCM initiative.

CHANGES TO MIDDLE SUPPLY MANAGEMENT

What happens to middle purchasing management, buyers, and agents who can't evolve into the SCM business ethic? As mentioned, middle supply managers assume different roles and have more accountability in SCM. If senior management considers middle purchasing agents or buyers frozen and unresponsive then obsolescent managers may be rightsized or whatever the current euphemism is for being fired. If middle supply managers can become flexible, then they prosper with more responsibility and authority.

What happens to first level purchasing supervision, the group of managers who are responsible for directing day-to-day supply operations? With the rise of employee involvement through self-managed, high-performance supply teams, the first-line purchasing supervisor has a new role. The supply supervisor supports problem-solving teams in his or her commodity or service area. The supervisor may become coach, facilitator, trainer, problem solver, assistant, motivator, or assume other roles. First-level supervision can make or break the SCM initiative.

SUMMARY

The best companies seem to have a culture that thrives on change - technology, customer, system, competitor, and marketplace changes. The faster the rate of change, the more these organizations thrive. It's a matter of anticipating customer requirements and leapfrogging the competition. These 'fast companies' seem to form supply confederations more easily than others.

In today's soft economy, it's difficult to promote supply development and improvement when there have been internal layoffs and supply reductions. The surviving employees may grieve for their departed compatriots. Suppliers may be worried about their own contracts and future. In this climate, a SCM initiative may be a euphemism for supply reduction. Supply chain stakeholders want assurance they will be part of the team next month.

What makes SCM especially difficult is that many supply chain details are unknown or deal with issues the supply manager cannot control, induce, or influence. In this atmosphere, the supply manager's role is even more challenging. As one supply manager once said to me, he could 'lead, follow, get out of the way, or be fired.'

CHAPTER 6:
SCM LEADERSHIP

As discussed in the last chapter, the single most difficult part of implementing a new management concept is getting the organization and its stakeholders to understand, accept, and embrace the need for change. Getting the support, commitment, and understanding of senior management is a significant hurdle for organizations implementing new management approaches.

CHIEF PURCHASING OFFICER (CPO)

Long range planning does not deal with future decisions but with the future of present decisions.
Peter F. Drucker

The Center for Advanced Purchasing Studies (CAPS) discovered that 37% of the surveyed companies created a chief purchasing position.[1]

FROM DIRECTOR TO VICE PRESIDENT

The fundamental premise of this book is that purchasing is evolving into supply management. The head purchasing position used to be a manager and sometimes a director. More often, companies are moving supply management to an executive level, chief purchasing officer (CPO).

We are now seeing VP's and above assuming the title of Chief Purchasing Officer or Chief Sourcing Officer. Titles are important because they reveal the importance an organization places on the function. The new chief purchasing officer may be an Executive Vice President, Senior Vice President or Vice President.

The CPO plays the mission critical role of providing 'make or buy' input, setting supply chain expectations, developing the SCM strategic vision/plan, communicating supply inducements, offering supply improvement assistance, and developing the supply base.

CPO VALUE PROPOSITION

The challenge of all organizations is the 'make or buy' decision. The CPO knows supply base capabilities and its ability to add strategic value. The CPO is brought into strategic discussions determining core competencies and what should be outsourced. Once a sourcing decision is made, the CPO provides the political will to make the hard and fast policies to whom, why, what, how, and when products will be outsourced.

CPO BACKGROUNDS

While many CPO's still come from purchasing, we are seeing changes. Since the supply management footprint is so broad and deep, non-sourcing professionals are bringing new processes, tools, and perspectives to supply management. In other words, it takes more than negotiating chops to cut it as a senior supply manager.

This isn't happening easily. I have heard a lot of grumbles from old line purchasing agents and buyers who say these new folks haven't paid their dues. I hear the following from traditional purchasing agents: "Do these new sourcing people have the savvy to sniff out supplier promises and make fundamental business decisions on expensive purchases?" These new people probably don't have the negotiating skills, relationships, and business skills of an old time sourcing pro. But, they bring new skills to the table such as being able to evaluate the effectiveness of a supplier's six-sigma program, incorporate the supplier's lean manufacturing initiative into the customers, and integrate the supplier's best design practices into the customer's product development.

THINK 'X'

What will the new SCM function look like? This is evolving. However, we can make some early observations. The supply manager is at the center of the supply chain, the point at which it is managed and controlled. But, it should be emphasized that this is only part of the supply chain equation. Supply chain stakeholders also include production control, quality engineering, design engineering, logistics, distribution, production scheduling, inventory management, demand forecasting, and customer follow up.

Visual models convey important information. The supply chain has often been shown as a horizontal series of linked boxes starting with the supplier and moving towards the final customer. Thomas T. Stallkamp, vice chairman and CEO, MSC International came up with a different visual. Instead of a horizontal chain, a vertical X with a pinch at the center better illustrates the role of supply management in the supply chain. Supply management is the control point of the supply chain - sharing plans, communicating demands, solving problems, monitoring quality/cost/delivery, and sharing information throughout the chain.[2]

SUPPLY CHAIN LEADERSHIP ROLES

Leadership is action, not position.
Donald McGannon

I thought about this for a long time. 'Succeed or perish' explains the prevalent thinking of most senior executives. This applies to the organization as well as to the senior management including CPO's. Think about it? There are no stupid, long-term senior managers. Most perish quickly upon making bad decisions.

HIGH IMPACT CPO ATTRIBUTES

What makes a CPO leader? Is a leader made, nurtured, or self selected? Leadership is still difficult to understand and to explain. More and more, leaders are seen as people who guide themselves or a group to do what needs to be done as well as reach ever-higher goals. In general, CPO's are normal people who possess high energy, are

---

CONTEXT: CPO Characteristics

- Flexible and adaptable.
- Excellent communicating abilities.
- Leadership by example.
- Persistent.
- Persuasive.
- Politically savvy.
- Relationship building abilities.
- Excellent planning and organization skills.
- Can do attitude.
- Cooperative.

---

committed, can share responsibility, have high values, and are highly credible.

The CPO is a leader who can learn and adapt to different circumstances. Another element of leadership is the ability to communicate at a visceral level. The CPO does not simply communicate supply information but also has the ability to communicate supply chain vision. Often, this communication means being actively involved in strategic and tactical discussions. The CPO questions, listens actively, and surfaces issues that are important to individuals, to supplier teams, and to the organization.

An interesting question is whether leadership can be learned and if it can be shared. Pursuing and sharing leadership seems to be a fundamental element of successful supply team problem solving and process improvement. Supply management teams have the responsibility and authority to ensure the supply chain runs smoothly. This message is deployed throughout the chain so critical stakeholders can improve their sub chain processes.

SUPPLY CHAIN LEADERSHIP AND MANAGEMENT ROLES

SCM requires new leadership and management abilities. Let's look at some of the new roles and responsibilities SCM requires:

- Visionary.

- Leader.

- Role model.

- Initiative or project sponsor.

- Change agent.

- Ombudsperson.

- Champion.

- Manager.

- Coach.

- Organizer.

- Mentor.

- Enabler.

- Cheerleader.

- Entrepreneur.

- Compliance officer.

- Translator.

- Engineer.

- System architect.

- Internal consultant.

Visionary

The CPO understands customer requirements and knows how to con-figure the supply base to satisfy these requirements. The CPO or senior supply manager must integrate supply base core competencies with those of the organization, direct the supply management function, and develop 'world class' suppliers. The CPO may have to redesign the supply management function and hire new supply managers who can develop, organize, motivate, coach, train, mentor, and energize suppliers. All of this requires vision.

Leader

Supply leadership and supply management may seem synonymous. However, leadership is an art. Depending on the requirements of the supply chain, market, organizational culture, and abilities of the people, leadership may involve 'command and control' or 'coaching and mentoring.' More often, supply leaders are closely involved with suppliers and employees, suggesting and demonstrating as opposed to directing what needs to be done.

Supply managers often must lead through example rather than through hierarchal or positional authority. As responsibilities and authorities have been downloaded to people actually doing the work, supply management functions have been downloaded to operating units. The supply manager may not be able to select a supplier or dictate a supply improvement initiative. Enlisting the support of supply chain stakeholders requires new management skills. The supply manager may have to lead by example and support operating personnel across functional areas and work processes. The supply manager must be able to develop relationships, trust, and credibility with operating managers.

Role Model

Integrity as a moral principle is often cited as a guide for personal and organizational performance. Integrity is also an essential element of all supply chain initiatives. The lack of integrity is the reason why many supply management initiatives have failed while others have flourished. Integrity is the ability to honor commitments with suppliers, customers, employees and other critical supply chain stakeholders. Integrity is the ethic that reinforces an organization's vision, mission and values.[3]

Initiative or Project Sponsor

A consistent mantra in this book is that a senior executive should sponsor the SCM initiative. In a large organization, the SCM sponsor may be the CPO who guides line supply managers. If supply management is new to the organization then the executive sponsor can:

- Provide access to senior management.

- Provide SCM resources.

- Handle major supply problems.

- Provide instant credibility to the SCM project and supply development initiative.

- Keep senior management informed of supply changes.

- Sit in on senior level meetings.

- Vocally and actively support the supply chain initiative.

Change Agent

Change agent is a relatively new term to describe the role of a person or a group to move the organization in a new direction. The CPO may be the organizational chain agent while supply managers may be the change agents for their commodity suppliers. Sometimes, the initial change agent is the CEO who assigns the supply transformational responsibilities to the CPO.

Usually a competitor initiates or a customer signals the need for change. Old ways of business are no longer sufficient to be competitive. For example, an organization may change from an engineering focused to a customer-focused supply chain organization. Or, it may have to evolve from a product, transaction orientation to a supply process orientation.

CONTEXT: Displaying SCM Leadership

- Align supply initiatives with the organizational strategic vision.
- Provide a clear direction and leadership for the function.
- Serve as a supply management role model.
- Empathize with the priorities and concerns of operating department heads and suppliers.
- Defer to others.
- Handle interpersonal conflicts effectively.
- Communicate clearly.
- Is a good listener.
- Present clear, useful, and doable information to senior management.
- Ensure efficient and effective stakeholder satisfaction.
- Focus on the business and organizational as well as the technical requirements of supply management.
- Is confident of skills and knowledge.
- Is creative and flexible.

Ombudsperson

In some organizations, the supply manager serves as the ombudsperson on critical supply chain issues. In much the same way, the human resources manager is the ombudsperson on organizational and cultural matters. The supply manager, as an ombudsperson, is the designated person to resolve quality, customer satisfaction, delivery, and customer-supply issues among teams, departments, and other business units.

Champion

The supply management champion may be the CPO, team of senior executives, or even the Chief Executive Officer. In formal and informal settings, the champion reminds the organization of the importance of supply management. The champion provides active and consistent support for SCM activities.

Manager

A supply manager has traditional managerial functions, specifically to:

- **Plan.** The supply manager communicates commodity, product and technical requirements to suppliers.

- **Organize.** The supply manager organizes the flow of information, and requirements to the supply base.

- **Control.** The supply manager establishes, monitors, and intervenes if required to correct supply processes.

- **Directs.** The supply manager directs and oversees supply team activities.

- **Staff.** The supply manager hires, develops, and evaluates supply staff performance.

Coach

The relationship between supply management and sports management is very close. Companies are evolving into groups of self-managed teams. Team structures are flat. The supply manager is more often a coach. The supply manager works through his or her employees. Coaching requires the ability to encourage teamwork, motivate employees, and establish direction.

In the athletic metaphor, the coach is nominally in charge. The coach decides who's on the team, who plays, and so on. But the coach isn't responsible for the big play or the series of downs that scores points. The coach broadly establishes the game plan, provides training, encourages self-sacrifice, mentors players, and serves other facilitating roles. Today's supply manager may well be the coach of the supply management team composed of multidisciplinary experts.

Supply managers and coaches have similar goals to be competitive and to win games. This requires getting the best from players. Success depends on how players follow through on supply management and development assignments.

Organizer

A major responsibility of the supply manager is to interface, organize, and monitor supply development and improvement projects. The supply manager may be responsible for organizing, facilitating, monitoring and reporting project progress. The supply manager also interfaces with operational units such as engineering, manufacturing, planning, and other functions to organize supply management activities.

Mentor

A supply manager must be a mentor and be capable of being mentored. For example, mentoring suppliers is fundamental to supply development and developing long-term supply relationships.

Enabler

The supply manager, as enabler, assists functional personnel and process owners to establish and meet their supply chain objectives. The enabler provides assistance and counsel to process owners and supply chain stakeholders. This may mean reviewing supply plans, evaluating product plans, monitoring supply processes, training supply personnel, monitoring improvement, and supporting supply management initiatives. The supply management enabler walks a fine line. The enabler can provide assistance and guidance but can't take responsibility away from process owners.

Cheerleader

Cheerleading managers are optimistically realistic. Cheerleading may involve a number of activities such as uplifting talks, encouraging supplier improvement teams, recognizing supplier accomplishments, thanking personnel, being a mentor, or defusing customer-supply tensions. They are infectious self-starters who generate enthusiasm in others. Cheerleader management isn't rose colored or Pollyannaish. Cheerleader management is tightly focused on raising awareness and pursuing supply chain improvement.

Supply chain cheerleaders focus energies on meeting the organization's business mission and objectives. They empower supply teams to target their energy and the company's resources on opportunities for success and high promise outcomes.

Cheerleading is one of the more difficult challenges for the supply manager. Disillusionment over a supply management initiative can take its toll. Cynicism or defeatism can result and become self-fulfilling. The supply manager must cheerlead when a project flags because of rising expectations, poor results, internal resistance, conflicting projects, ego-gratification, selfishness, poor communications, or slow SCM progress.

Entrepreneur
Several years ago, there was a trend to outsource purchasing functions. Internal users became customers. Purchasing departments became service departments. They had to become customer, cost, and value sensitive. The supply management function became a small business and the supply manager became an entrepreneur. Supply management billed user departments for supply training, consulting, management, and other services. These services had to add value and be competitively priced. Purchasing had to compete directly with external providers of the same services. This ensured internal staff provided value. If operating groups didn't want to use the supply department's services, the message was loud and clear - no business, no monies, no purchasing personnel.

Compliance Officer
Every manager is aware of workplace regulations such as sexual harassment, equal opportunity, and disability. Federal and state regulations impact almost every element of the supply chain involving packaging, safety, health, and so on. Minority and other disadvantaged sourcing issues are also among the most sensitive public purchasing challenges.

Translator

Each discipline has its own language including mechanical engineering, supply management, finance, and sales. The language of supply management is a process based driven language involving lean, six sigma, just in time, ERP and other supply concepts.

Engineer

Supply managers are more often being pulled into new product development. Since supply managers must find the most capable supply-partners to bring into product development, supply managers of high tech products often have some technical background. This helps supply managers who are given a heads up of required materials, components, and services and must source long-lead technical products.

System Architect

The supply manager may have to architect the supply process chain. The supply manager has to work with stakeholders to reengineer processes, information flows, technical systems and other processes. The conventional wisdom is that companies must transform processes and streamline work flows to become globally competition. Supply chain redesign is a never-ending process to accommodate new products or satisfy new customer requirements.

Internal Consultant

The supply management function is often a staff function. The function may have few full time employees and a small budget. The department must leverage itself through operating departments to get the job done. The supply management department may not have the staff to support major supply management and development initiatives, such as ISO 9001:2015, lean, six sigma quality, customer-supply partnering.

As more supply management responsibilities are operationalized, what is the role of the supply manager? The supply manager may become an internal consultant. The manager works with operational groups, suppliers, process owners, and plant managers to initiate supply initiatives and install control mechanisms to ensure a smooth flow of

> ### CONTEXT: Matrix Organization Benefits
>
> - Shared authority and responsibility.
> - Team access to organizational resources.
> - Responsiveness to customers.
> - Conflicts resolved quickly.
> - Information and resource availability.
> - Job security and availability for team members.
> - Rapid response time.
> - Rapid deployment of specialists and team members.
> - Use of multidisciplinary resources.
> - Shared knowledge, skills, and other resources.

products. This role requires a special individual who has 'real world' consulting expertise. A supply chain consultant must be a self-starter and be able to discover opportunities for improvement and innovation.

SUPPLY CHAIN ORGANIZATION

Draw them (organizational charts) in pencil. Never formalize, print, and circulate them.
Robert Townsend, CEO, Avis

APICS defines supply chain management as "the planning, organizing, and controlling of supply chain activities."[4] So, the question arises what's the best structure to organize the function?

SEARCHING FOR THE BEST ORGANIZATIONAL STRUCTURE

In the last 20 years, a number of organizational structures have been introduced. These include: traditional-hierarchical, matrix, virtual, etc. Is there one best structure? No. The appropriate supply chain structure is one that supports a group of people who can work together to satisfy customers and meet business objectives using the fewest resources possible. Within this structure, congruent, and supportive systems are created that reinforce the organizational culture.

The traditional form of business organization is hierarchal. However, a supply process chain implies a horizontal, integrated process. Innovative supply chain organizations models are springing up based on interlocking groups, virtual partnerships, strategic alliances, and matrix organizations.

MATRIX ORGANIZATIONS

Matrix organizations became popular in the 60s and 70s as a way to satisfy internal customers and multiple stakeholders. Matrix organizations have been especially popular in aerospace and high tech supply chain organizations. In the traditional aerospace matrix organization, special procurement projects usually had multiple reporting structures.

A matrix organization is just what the name implies. A matrix supply management reporting structure overlays the traditional functional structure. Supply project teams report up and across the organizational structure. Their work may take them up and down the supply chain. Authority and responsibility for a project is shared among several groups. This structure works well with supply management teams but has problems when it becomes institutionalized. Several disadvantages to matrix structures include reporting and responsibility ambiguities, implementation conflicts, and additional costs.

Multidisciplinary customer-supply teams also blend well with a matrix organization. The supply team may have multiple reporting routes. A supply chain improvement team may report to the supply chain function and to a line organization where the improvement project is being conducted. As well, individual multidisciplinary team members may report to different organizational areas.

Supply management teams succeed in a matrix organization because:

- Team leader understands organizational culture.

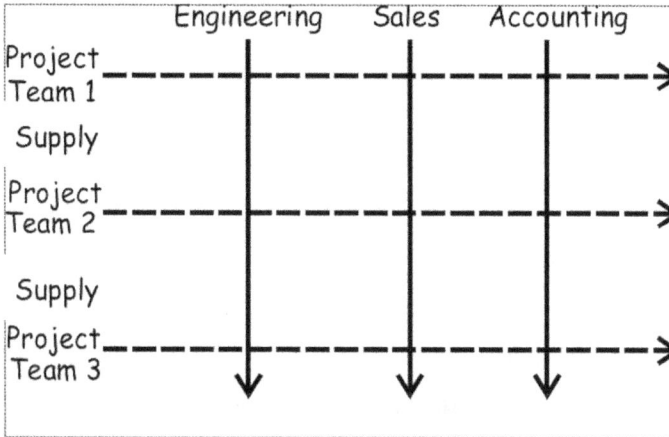

- Team members understand requirements.

- Team members are loyal.

- Commitments are made and followed.

- Conflict resolution is fair and quick.

- Good communication channels exist horizontally and vertically.

- Everyone participates in the planning process.

VIRTUAL ORGANIZATIONS

In today's lean and mean competitive times, key skills are retained through supply partnerships, which result in the growth of virtual organizations. The virtual organization is an amorphous entity that delivers products or services to customers with the external appearance of a single company or supply chain. In much the same way, virtual supply chains will become more prevalent as more small suppliers develop state-of-the-art, world-class competencies, skills, technologies, capabilities, information or other resources. These unique assets are pooled and integrated with other companies to form an integrated network of turnkey supply capabilities. When the contract is over, the virtual supply chain disbands.

CONTEXT: Matrix Organization Challenges

- Communication and coordination conflicts.
- No or little administrative support.
- Conflicts with operating groups.
- Multiple reporting paths.
- Multiple work flow paths.
- Possibility of changing priorities.
- Simultaneous and conflicting projects.
- Possibility of control and power conflicts.
- High overhead due to parallel costs.
- Additional organizational layers.
- Group think.
- Excessive management.
- Decision making by consensus.
- Multiple and maybe conflicting policies and procedures.

Examples of virtual organizations include: supply chains, global consulting organizations, franchising, joint ventures, and strategic alliances. What pulls everyone together in the virtual supply chain is synergy - the awareness that the sum of supplier skills and knowledge is greater than the individual parts.

To make the virtual chain work, supply-partners must bring something of value to the table. It may be special knowledge, special design capabilities, or other resources. When the project is over, the virtual supply group may develop another product or the group may disband. The advantages of the virtual chain include: low overhead, low risks, flexibility, and improved overall supply performance.

THE ORCHESTRA AS SUPPLY EXCELLENCE METAPHOR

The orchestra as well as an athletic team is often used as a metaphor for supply chain excellence. The orchestra is a group of individuals, each of whom has a unique talent and a distinct way of delivering customer satisfaction. Usually, each player is a superstar in his or her right.

Each musician as an individual and an orchestra player adds value and pleasure to the theatergoer.

The parallels to supply chain excellence are strong. Each orchestra musician or supplier is chosen because of unique abilities and talents. The musician or supplier must pass an audition based on talent and ability. Once the musician or supplier is chosen, the musician must practice, rehearse, and continue to build upon his or her abilities, much like a supply-partner.

The orchestra is composed of different instruments and sections. This is similar to any supply chain with its functional groups, professionals, processes, and teams. The goal of each musical section, whether it is woodwinds, strings, or brass is to be consistent but also blend with other musical sections. Each professional may also add his or her own interpretation to the music much as a supply-partner may develop core capabilities and provide entire systems or assemblies.

The orchestra conductor, movie director, or supply manager is more often a team leader and coach than an authoritarian manager. The conductor or supply manager leads a group of professionals who are proficient with their instruments and have core abilities. The role of the modern conductor is to interpret the musical score and to shape the orchestra's sound so it pleases the audience. In the supply chain, the supply manager fine-tunes the supply stream so the customer is satisfied with the delivered product or service. The supply manager, much like the conductor, leads by interpretation, example, and strength of personality rather than by edict.[5]

INTERNAL CROSS FUNCTIONAL COLLABORATION

A *Industry Week Magazine* survey noted that supply chain collaboration is essential to achieving world-class results.[6]

Key process owners are responsible for their work output. The supply manager should be sensitive to these requirements. The supply manager may have different objectives than the line manager or core process owner. The line manager is under daily pressure to maintain process stability, keep customers satisfied, keep production up, improve performance, and meet regulatory requirements. The line manager isn't responsible for upstream or downstream production. The result is that supply chain priorities may fall by the way side. So, a major responsibility of the supply manager is to monitor overall supply chain process flows while being sensitive to operational realities.

Operational and supply managers must deal on a daily basis with the following:

- Conflicting customer requirements and messages.

- Demanding and irritable customers.

- Personnel issues.

- Regulatory constraints.

- Safety issues.

- Lack of resources.

- Spikes or troughs in demand.

- Process breakdowns.

- Personnel turnover.

- Grievances and other personnel challenges.

Supply management also may have limited resources. The department may have a small full time and a part time staff. The part time staff may be borrowed experts from production planning, manufacturing, quality engineering, or design engineering. These people usually report dotted line to supply management but are direct reports to their functional department or area. For example, supply management may facilitate and project manage the process. Quality may provide a person to assist in supplier auditing, certification, and product testing. The human

CONTEXT: Rolling Stones Tour

The Rolling Stones tour is an example of a virtual, projectized supply chain organization. The Rolling Stones tour brought together an international team of architects, stage movers, lighting technicians, sound technicians, pilots, camera crews, truck drivers, security, and other personnel to operate the Rolling Stone's tour for 16 months.

The tour was a monster by any comparison. There were three different stages, each of which weighted 170 tons. Fifty-six trailers and three jumbo cargo planes transported the stages. The stages were rotated while one was being used, one was being dismantled, and a third was being erected.

Why was the tour a virtual corporation or project? The tour was not meant to be permanent because it had a one-year life expectancy. People, resources, and equipment gathered in each city, operated in a synchronized fashion, and when the tour ended, the tour team disbanded.

Each person, a supplier, brought a specialized skill to the tour so there was just-in-time assembly and delivery of a concert in a different city each night. Skills were purchased or contracted as required. Each person was a professional. There was no headquarters building, just a core group of people who knew what to do when and how to coordinate all the activities.[7]

resources function may provide training or team facilitators for special projects. Production may provide first line supervisors to assist in conducting FMEA, SPC, or capability studies. Engineering may provide experts who develop technical specifications.

SUPPLY MANAGEMENT AS PROJECT MANAGEMENT

Every supply manager knows the expression 'on time, on budget, and satisfied stakeholders'. This is mission critical to all sourcing, materials, and logistics professionals. Well, these three issues: on time relates to delivery schedule, on budget relates to overall contract cost, and satisfied customers relate to scope and quality. Cost, quality and schedule are the primary legs of project management. The conclusion is simple. Supply managers are also project managers.

In many ways, the supply manager is evolving into a project manager. The product or service being sourced has a contract, product, or project lifecycle. The project lifecycle starts with identifying customer needs, developing a project definition, and ending with the termination of the contract. It starts all over again with a new product to be sourced. And throughout the contract, product or project life cycle, the supply manager addresses new contract terms, contract changes, and manages communications.

CORE PROCESS WORK MODEL

Successful big corporations should devolve into becoming 'confederations of entrepreneurs.
Norman McCrae, Editor

The outsourcing and supply management phenomena have created significant problems within organizations. The *Economist Magazine* summed it up neatly:

> "Focusing on core competencies might mean outsourcing peripheral employees, but it also means creating a core group of loyal employees who have worked for the company for years; who have absorbed or helped to create its ethos; and who are committed enough to transmit that ethos to future employees. … the focus is increasingly on finding non-financial carrots to retain these 'core 'employees (if the only reason why an employee stays with any particular firm is money, then he or she is much easier to poach."[8]

The 'outsourcing' concept originally dealt with buying products from external suppliers. 'Outsourcing' now has become synonymous with

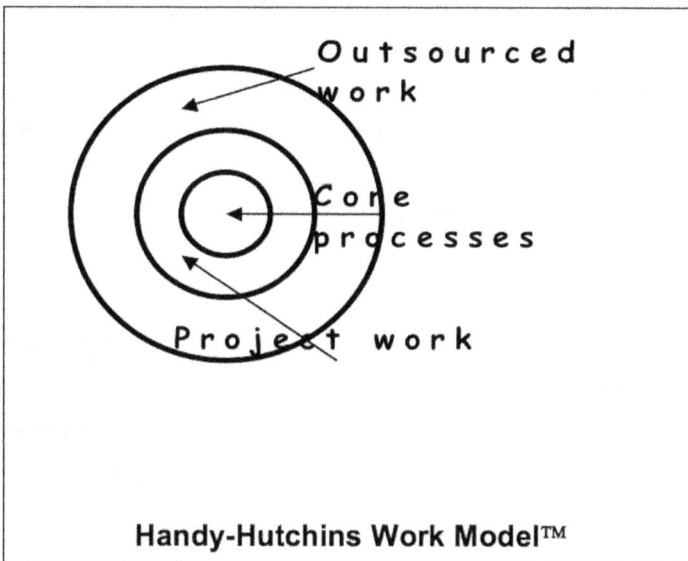

Handy-Hutchins Work Model™

people losing their jobs. The rationale can be understood through the Handy/Hutchins Work Model.™

Charles Handy, probably today's smartest workplace guru, said more than twenty years ago that work is fundamentally changing. He developed a visual model of work based on three concentric circles, which we expanded upon:

- **Inner ring**. The inner ring consists of the organization's core competencies that distinguish it from the competition. The core process owners are in charge of the organizational future – keeping an eye on the competition, on new markets, and on strategy. The center is also in charge of the organization's overall architecture, specifically how it does work.[9] The inner ring is composed of corporate insiders, supply managers, and professionals. They are the glue that holds the organization together and grows it. These insiders may be highly trained executives, professionals, marketing strategists, design engineers, supply managers, and accountants who sustain the institutional memory. These full-time employees define the organization's vision, mission, principles, culture, and ethics.

- **Middle ring.** Middle ring is composed of project workers who support the organizational core processes. Project workers can be full time employees, contractors or temporary workers. I call these project people because they're mainly involved in discrete projects with a definite beginning and end. These people provide special skills, knowledge, and abilities that add organizational value.[10]

- **Outer ring.** Outer ring work is composed of largely interchange-able contract workers. These workers are often less-skilled ser-vice employees. Many are marginal workers who service the repetitive needs of the organization such as food service, admin-istrative chores, or travel services.[11]

Does this work model reflect how supply chains are organized? For example, a company may want to develop a complex new product. The company doesn't have internal resources so it will complement its core team with contractor-specialists or with key supply-partners with com-plementary skills. Or, if a fast-food restaurant anticipates a spring or summer rush of business, it will hire temps to ensure there are sufficient people to prepare food and service customers.

IT COMES DOWN TO PEOPLE

Experience is a hard teacher because she gives the test first, the lesson afterwards.
Vernon Law, Professional Baseball Player

As the velocity of technology increases, supply management organiza-tions must adapt and anticipate these changes. The essence of an or-ganization and its supply chain is constantly being challenged. Compa-nies, organizations, and institutions have a body of culture, values, prin-ciples, and infrastructure that seem to value the status quo in direct challenge to the acceleration of technology.

While purchasing is sometimes considered middle ring work, supply management roles, authorities, responsibilities are definitely migrating from the middle ring to the inner core. More companies recognize their supply chains are an untapped opportunity to impact the bottom line and gain competitive advantage.

MOVING TO THE CORE

Frankly, the Handy/Hutchins work model is a real organizational challenge to find, retain and motivate the best supply managers. As Handy said:

> "The old model of the corporation was a piece of property, a piece of real estate. It was, quite simply, the property of its owners. … The new model is based on an understanding that to hold people inside the corporation, we can't really talk about them being employees anymore. To hold people, there has to be some continuity and sense of belonging. We also have to talk about two-way commitment – corporation to member, member to corporation"[12]

The Handy/Hutchins work model is devilishly simple. It provides the rationale to outsource non-core activities. When Handy first proposed his vision of the corporate workplace, it was considered too bleak and radical. Middle managers were considered indispensable. Many professionals and functions were considered necessary to sustain the organization. This has now all changed. All organizations are asking: "What's core and what's not." Core functions are retained while non-core activities are outsourced.

Purchasing was considered a non-core, clerical, and transactional function. Now, the competitive imperative of supply chain management has moved it to the core. Supply management is considered indispensable to an organization's competitiveness and profitability.

FINDING AND RETAINING GREAT SUPPLY MANAGERS

Developing organizational core competencies more often today involves finding, nurturing, and rewarding the 'best and brightest' employees. These are the organization's entrepreneurs, innovators, and dreamers. They are the people who create organizational and market value.

The 'best and brightest' supply managers are the means for actualizing supply chain processes. In today's talent wars, companies are competing to find and keep these people. These high potential supply managers are induced through high salaries and generous options. The goal isn't corporate paternalism but entrepreneurism where each supply manager has the opportunity to reach his or her potential and be accordingly rewarded. The hope for results included high retention, positive morale, exceptional loyalty, and intelligent risk taking.

The *Economist Magazine* distilled the importance of securing 'the best and brightest' supply managers:

> "With the life-cycle of products shrinking and competition coming from unexpected corners of the globe, companies have to be more nimble than ever. This uncertainty helps some workers: if a firm has no idea from which direction the next competitive threat will come, one of its few sensible strategies is to amass good people to prepare for as many contingencies as possible."[13]

SUPPLY MANAGEMENT TEAMS

Very small groups of highly skills generalists show a remarkable propensity to succeed.
Ramchandran Jaikumar

Supply managers have to learn new skills to be successful in the 'supply chain of the future' where integrated factories and suppliers instantaneously communicate to control processes and monitor products.

We believe that within a few years, more highly trained, technical workers will fill many supply management positions. Why? The consequences of supply chain failure are so high that the profession will require a diverse and technology friendly group of supply management professionals. If supply chain or plant managers need information, they will tap directly into central computers without any need of middle managers to collect, integrate, and communicate the information.

ANATOMY OF KILLER SCM TEAMS

Supply management teams come in many shapes and forms. Teams can be loose clusters of individuals or they can be highly structured, customer-supply project teams bound by contracts and mutual obligations. They can be self-managed or can be tightly controlled. They can be permanent or temporary. A team's shape is flexible depending on skills, purpose, objectives, culture, company politics, technology, and a number of other factors.

Quinn Mills in **The Rebirth of the Corporation** describes the new organization as clusters of teams that share the following:

- Handle their own administrative functions.

- Develop their own expertise.

- Express a strong customer orientation.

- Are project and action oriented.

- Share information broadly.

- Accept accountability for business results.[14]

USE OF MULTI-SKILLED SUPPLY MANAGEMENT TEAMS

There are many types of customer-supply project teams. An executive project team may develop a supply chain strategy. Divisional or business unit teams may negotiate a partnering arrangement with suppliers, develop customer-supply procedures, implement elements of a supply chain initiative, or develop procedures to improve supplier quality. Plant level teams may pursue ISO 9001:2015 registration, monitor incoming products, or integrate a new machine into the production line.

Entire supply chains are now structured in self-managed supply teams. To realize the potential of technology, organizations are integrating supply chain stakeholders into these multiskilled teams. In these systems, semiautonomous teams of five to seven multiskilled stakeholders work on issues spread across the chain. Teamwork, participative managers, and multiskilled workers are keys to success. The payoff is supply management designed around participative and innovative teams is 30-50% more productive than conventional methods of organizing work.[15]

Self-managed supply teams share common goals and accept responsibility for production schedules, quality, cost control, upgrading professional skills and assignment of work. Previously, purchasing may have been responsible for these activities. Now, multidisciplinary supply teams direct these activities.

END OF THE LONE RANGER

The lone ranger is dead in all organizations - the lone person developing killer software, the lone salesperson selling million dollar systems, or the lone CPO visioning the future of a billion-dollar supply chain. No one person has the skills to inspire and know all things. There is too much diversity and access to resources and information. No one person is as smart as a motivated team.

An example may help to illustrate this point. In the supply chain, work is arranged around end-to-end processes, rather than specific tasks. A semiautonomous supply management team of five to seven multiskilled stakeholders may manage a process that spans across several functional departments and goes out into the supply stream. Functional specialists from engineering, sourcing, or manufacturing engineering may participate or support this team on an as needed basis. Supply chain problem solving requires broad based jobs, teamwork, participative managers, and multiskilled workers.

SUMMARY

Supply managers must evolve and adopt new roles. Supply managers have more authority and are more visible than traditional purchasing managers. The profession is also attracting more highly trained and educated personnel. Companies often require supply managers to have engineering and other degrees, professional certifications, and be cross-trained. Experience in product development/design engineering allows supply professionals to challenge supplier's specifications, which may be restrictive from a sourcing point of view. Operations and design experience allow supply professionals to obtain the respect of manufacturing personnel while providing input to design and quality decisions.

We're also going to see more CPO's with non-sourcing backgrounds. They bring a new enterprise and process perspective to the supply management function. They understand business objectives, organizational processes, technology integration, and supply chain methodologies. The bottom line is that sourcing professionals are going be more well rounded. This cuts to the fundamental issue: "What's your future in the supply management profession?"

CHAPTER 7:
SCM TOOLS AND TECHNIQUES

In this chapter, we discuss SCM tools and techniques.

Supply chain management has become an umbrella of diverse methods, principles, and ideas. Cycle time management, just in time (JIT)
management, lean management, quality management, benchmarking,
and logistics management are all fundamental elements, tools and techniques of supply chain management.

CYCLE TIME MANAGEMENT
Manage the opportunities change offers.
Advertisement.

Time is a critical element of supply chain competitiveness. Since customer needs change so quickly, the speed by which a company re-
sponds affects its reputation, credibility, and profitability. Cycle time
management is the analysis, control, and reduction of how long it takes
to do something critical.

THE ACCELERATION OF CHANGE
Business hurdles and barriers are higher than five years ago. In only
several years, low price and high quality products and services can't
guarantee success anymore. Products must be developed and delivered quickly to satisfy fickle customer tastes. As well, risks throughout
the supply chain are higher. Customers want the right cost-competitive,
customized products quickly.

Change is occurring at an increasing rate. What is the role of supply management amidst this change? Organizations are struggling streamline their internal supply management processes and upgrade the supply management function to reflect its new strategic importance.

THE POWER OF FIRST

The first company often has a dramatic market advantage. The list of firsts are extensive - first to market, first to implement SCM processes, first to win the Baldrige Performance Excellence Program, first to implement just-in-time systems, and first to deliver a product to market. Markets are fragmented with customers with diverse needs who want them fulfilled instantly with products or processes that not only exceed their expectations but even astonish them.

A company that can satisfy diverse customers with lower cost, high value products and services delivered just in time and in the right manner has a higher probability of beating its competition. Delivering products and services faster requires a company does the right things right the first time and every time. The overall value-add culture must be ingrained in the organization. Supply chain processes are standardized, proceduralized, stabilized, and capable. Everyone is trained to do their jobs right. All supply chain, non-value added processes and systems are eliminated.

CYCLE TIME REDUCTION

Innovation and technology drive the supply chain model. Think Moore's Law, which basically says computer chip processing power doubles every 18 to 24 months. Now apply this to the supply chain. We're seeing this in almost every industry. For example, high-powered computers allow automakers to design two vehicles in the time they spent on designing one and do it in half the time.[1]

Motorola reorganized its semiconductor business because of increasing customer requirements. Traditionally, Motorola designed and manufactured generic computer chips for different markets. Now, Motorola zeroes in on critical customer requirements so it can turn out a product in 30 days instead of three or more months.[2]

CRITICAL CYCLE TIME REDUCTION AREAS

Cycle time reduction throughout the supply chain is critical to resolving chronic problems; improving customer deliveries; responding to fashions, trends, and tastes; eliminating waste; responding to product recalls; implementing new sourcing processes, and introducing new products to market.

Time as a competitive advantage is illustrated in the following examples:

- Product development partnerships.

- Just-in-time production.

- Just-in-time delivery.

Product Development Partnerships

Time to market, first to market, and first to critical mass are key product development metrics. Few companies have the ability to create by themselves the products they need to be globally competitive and to satisfy all their customers.

Large companies are now scanning the horizon for small companies with new ideas, lots of energy, and special skills they want but don't have. Sometimes, large companies will buy smaller, entrepreneurial companies. Sometimes, large companies will license technology or partner with smaller companies. These supply chain partnerships are called strategic alliances, joint ventures, strategic partnerships, or even virtual corporations. They exist as long as each partner adds value and as long as revenues are produced.

Just-in-Time Production

Just-in-time (JIT) production or manufacturing is the systematic elimination of waste throughout the product or service delivery stream. Just in time starts internally and is then driven through the supply chain. The goal of JIT is to eliminate all waste. Superfluous raw material, extra material handling, inventory, extra labor, and inadequate supervision add unnecessary costs to the process.

Just-in-Time Delivery

The marketplace changes quickly. New competitors arise. Customers are fickle. Customers want products delivered over night. In general, everything in business seems to accelerate at electronic speed. The windows of opportunity are shrinking as supply chain stakeholders are linked electronically. Parts must be delivered just in time for assembly or test. Inventories are held down to close to zero. The time between a customer order and product delivery is reduced to a minimum. Products across the world are delivered within 24 hours of being ordered.

JUST IN TIME MANAGEMENT

The first person gets the oyster; the second person gets the shell.
Andrew Carnegie, businessperson

Lean management, quality management, benchmarking management, logistics management, and just in time management are complementary concepts. The goals of all BTO and JIT processes are to eliminate waste, add value, and optimize the entire chain of value added activities from understanding customer requirements to quickly delivering a product. In this section, we refer to these practices by the more traditional JIT term.

ROCKS IN THE LAKE

Just in time (JIT) is a broad philosophy covering many operational areas. Just in time broadly is the design and management of customer-supply, value-added processes to minimize cycle and lead times. The precise arrival of parts to the specific location is the conventional interpretation of just in time. However, it is but one example of the very broad impact of JIT.

JIT is often illustrated as rocks in a stream or as a giant iceberg. As water is lowered or inventory is reduced, more chronic problems are discovered which must be corrected. Inventory hides operational problems including machine downtime, scrap, work in process buffer inventories, engineering design redundancies, change orders, inspection backlog, paper backlog, poor material quality, high scrap rates, late supplier deliveries, transaction errors, double orders, safety stock, and rejected materials.

JIT MANAGEMENT ELEMENTS

JIT broadly incorporates a number of SCM techniques and tools, specifically:

- **Just-in-time deliveries.** Products are delivered just in time to be used on the manufacturing floor. Deliveries are in small quantities, supplied more frequently, and have an exact count.

- **Suppliers located close to the plant.** In order that shipments are delivered reliably, suppliers of perishable, critical, or heavy products are located near the customer's plant.

- **High quality goods.** JIT delivery requires supplied products are defect free. If defective products end up on the customer's production line then the line will stop until the defective products are replaced.

- **Reengineered internal and supply processes.** Internal processes are examined and if necessary redesigned. Streamlined processes add value and eliminate waste, which are the core values of all just-in-time processes.

- **Total quality.** Total quality in its broadest sense is the goal and objective of every value-adding, process stream. Total quality involves all elements from astonishing customers to ensuring products conform to specifications.

- **Controlled and capable processes.** Critical supply chain processes are stable and capable. Stable processes are in control.

Capable processes meet or exceed customer requirements. The goal of all controlled and capable processes is to eliminate unwanted variation.

- **Customer-supply partnering.** An important element in JIT is the need for fewer suppliers. Multiple product suppliers result in increased product, delivery, cost, and quality variation caused by lack of understanding, poor communication, or differences in capabilities. Whatever the cause, the results are the same - poor quality products and services result in dissatisfied customers.

- **Workers and management commit to work together.** The entire JIT process from order taking to product/service delivery is streamlined. Many disparate parts of the organization must work together as smoothly as an expensive Swiss watch. If there are problems, they are root cause solved and eliminated.

- **Dock to production delivery.** Dock-to-stock was the prevailing JIT wisdom for many years. Now, companies want to eliminate all inventories - incoming, buffer, and final inventories - and move incoming parts directly onto the production line or to the point of sale.

- **Sequenced delivery.** The right parts have to arrive at the right location in the proper amount, at the right time, and in the right order. Even the packing of the parts in a truck or railcar is critical. For example, parts are packed in the truck in the reverse order in which they will be unloaded. To minimize handling and storage, parts are pulled from the truck in the sequence they will be used on the assembly line. There are a number of benefits to sequenced delivery. Trucks can be unloaded quickly. Parts go directly onto the production line. Trucks don't have to wait to unload. Costs are reduced. Queues are eliminated. Space isn't required to repalettize or shift parts. Loading dock efficiency is increased.

- **Proper packaging.** Parts have to be packaged suitably for use. If parts are packaged loosely then products can be damaged. If parts are packaged too robustly then additional personnel, equipment and time are required to break down the packaging.

- **Accurate demand forecasting.** Forecasting is one of the most critical activities in SCM. Without accurate forecasts, supply chain partners can only react to orders as they are received. With constantly increasing pressure to reduce lead times, this means large inventories at various points along the supply chain. With good demand forecasts, shared with supply partners, these 'just in case' inventories can be significantly reduced.

- **Accurate price forecasting.** Supply managers must also develop supply availability and price forecasts. Frequently, much time and effort are devoted to developing demand forecasts, but forecasts of supply capabilities to keep up with increasing orders are often overlooked. Without them, however, parts may not arrive in sufficient quantities. Similarly, as supply segments approach capacity, prices are likely to escalate. Both conditions are critical and must be forecasted accurately.

JUST IN TIME SUPPLY MANAGEMENT

Just in time assumes a smooth process flow of products. Let's say that a supplier gets an order of 100 parts one day and the next day it increases to 200 or even more. How is this order going to be fulfilled? Is the supplier going to work two shifts to fulfill the order? Or, is the supplier going to pull products from inventory? Both responses violate several principles of lean and just in time management.

The solution to this significant problem is to control variation through long term sourcing and partnering relationships. The number of suppliers is reduced and streamlined so that some may be a single supplier while others are part of a select group of commodity suppliers. The purchase agreements may last for years. There are strong bonds

---

CONTEXT: The Seven Deadly Wastes

- **Motion:** incorrect layout of office and factory, lack of proximity of machines, off-line resources.
- **Waiting Time:** lack of coordination, idle operators watching a machine, long set-ups.
- **Overproduction:** inaccurate forecast, large batches, full utilization of machines and labor.
- **Processing:** poor machine maintenance, unnecessary processing steps.
- **Defects:** rework, troubleshooting delays, dissatisfied downstream customers.
- **Inventory:** space requirements, obsolescence, clutter, lack of forecast accuracy.
- **Transportation:** unnecessary movement of material, extra handling.[3]

---

between the manufacturer and supply-partner with each depending on the other for profitability.

JUST-IN-TIME AND SCM METRICS

Just-in-time metrics cover a number of SCM dimensions, such as:

- Timeliness.

- Reliability.

- Product integrity.

- Customer service.

- Accurate and complete information.

- Flexibility.

Timeliness

Timeliness is the ability to deliver a product when and where the customer wants it. Cycle time management and speed are the keys to JIT delivery. Especially in JIT distribution, the internal customer wants products delivered onto the production line at precise schedules.

Reliability

Reliability is the ability to deliver products at scheduled intervals. Delivery reliability is measured in terms of transit time, which is compared to promised delivery. Supply management can contract for supplies to be drop shipped on a monthly basis at a specific location. The manufacturer relies on the supplier to meet delivery obligations every month; otherwise a missed shipment shuts the production line. If missed shipments become a habit, then the customer is required to carry additional inventory to meet unexpected demands. This is expensive because of high inventory, storage, and handling costs.

Product Integrity

Product integrity means a defect-free product is delivered intact to the customer. There is no storage, shipping, or handling damage. Once delivered, the product functions as the customer expects.

Customer Service

Customer service keeps the customer advised of delivery problems, providing notice of product changes and price changes, providing accurate invoicing, satisfying warranty claims, reconciling billing differences, and supplying technical assistance.

The sales engineer provides current and accurate information of a product's special features, maintenance history, and performance levels. An order desk clerk provides prompt and efficient order taking. If product integrity has been compromised, then problems need to be resolved courteously, quickly, and satisfactorily.

Accurate and Complete Information

Product delivery isn't complete if support documentation isn't current, accurate, and complete. This is especially important for a complex industrial product. Support documentation includes product certifications, parts lists, engineering prints, spares list, operating instructions, maintenance instructions, inspection reports, and other product information.

Flexibility

Flexibility is the ability to respond to sudden customer needs. For example, a customer requires a rush delivery to satisfy unexpected demands. Sudden needs may require substituting material, rescheduling shipments, or changing carriers.

JIT ADVANTAGES

JIT management is fundamental to supply chain management. JIT is different than traditional distribution management. In JIT, material distribution, transportation, storage, and handling are synchronized to ensure reliable and stable product delivery. Customer inventory is reduced drastically and is hopefully eliminated. Product warehousing requirements are also reduced.

Specifically, JIT management result in:

- Fewer suppliers.

- Improved product quality.

- Reduced inventory.

- Fewer nonproductive personnel.

- Lower costs.

Fewer Suppliers

JIT requires fewer suppliers. JIT requirements ultimately reduce the supplier list to those that can comply with contractual commitments. Compliant suppliers are offered inducements, such as predictable orders for their products. Suppliers of critical products are often the most compliant, willing to learn, and try new techniques. These suppliers have major accounts and have the largest incentive to adopt new management practices.

Improved Product Quality

Quality, as 100% conforming material shipments, is required for the proper functioning of JIT. The customer does not inspect any incoming material shipments. If a supplier delivers a shipment with defective products, then the customer's production line stops. Other production lines down the supply chain also stop. This is expensive. Once suppliers understand the consequences of failure, they must deliver on time, defect-free material.

Reduced Inventory

The goal of JIT management is to progressively reduce all types of inventory. Traditionally, by maintaining high inventory levels, a supplier could provide a high level of customer service by supplying products on demand. Inventory was a buffer to balance unpredictable supply and demand levels.

Fewer Nonproductive Personnel

As inventories are reduced, the number of material handlers, parts inspectors, supervisors, and other employees, who don't add read supply chain value are reduced.

Lower Costs

The SCM goal is to lower overall costs. JIT management, regardless of what it's called works because it impacts the bottom line. Nissan Motor estimated that converting to a just in time integrated supply chain saves up to $3,600 per vehicle. This is more than the net profit realized from each vehicle.[4]

JIT SUCCESS

JIT drastically reduces investment as well as total supply chain costs. In the 1990s, the U.S. automobile industry quickly realized the advantages of JIT. U.S. automakers were carrying $775 worth of work-in-process inventory for each car they built, while the Japanese carried only $150. The very existence of the U.S. auto industry depended on adopting the JIT philosophy. We are now in the same predicament as companies became fat, inventories rose, and quality has plummeted in many sectors over the last decade.

Delphi Automotive Systems, a GM supplier, is another JIT success story. It used lean and JIT management to increase business performance. Productivity was up 200% in one facility, lead time for deliveries were reduced by 50%, late shipments at premium rates were down 15% and inventory turn improved by 170%.[5]

LEAN MANAGEMENT

Nothing is more satisfying when timing and delivery occur in perfect sequence.
Anonymous

Lean management or simply 'lean' is now the hot buzzword. In the *Industry Week* survey, 55% of corporate executives identified lean manufacturing as 'extremely critical' to their ability to become world class.[6]

WHAT IS LEAN?

The question is what is 'lean' and how should it be implemented within the supply chain? Lean incorporates many SCM and JIT management ideas such as sequenced delivery, to lower inventory levels, and quick changing machine set up times.

The following are common definitions of 'lean':

> "a philosophy of manufacturing that focuses on delivering the highest value product at the lowest cost on time."[7]

> "a systematic approach to identifying and eliminating waste (nonvalue added activities) through continuous improvement ..."[8]

Many SCM ideas are evolving into a philosophy of thinking lean and working lean. Lean first focused on manufacturing and the concept is now morphing to include the entire supply value stream consisting of all steps needed to convert resources into products or services the customer wants. Any process steps that costs too much, takes too long or doesn't optimize value is wasteful and is eliminated.

STARTED WITH TOYOTA

Many just in time and lean ideas originated at Toyota Motor Company. The principal idea was to foster flexible, low-cost and shorter production runs that could meet customer requirements for high quality, low cost products. Now take this idea and apply it throughout the supply chain. This is the intent of lean supply management. Does it work? It is more difficult that it looks. Design, production, and parts ordering must be seamless and smooth.

LEAN INITIATIVES

Let's look at lean initiatives at Boeing, Daimler-Benz, and Johnson Controls. When reading these stories notice how lean integrates quality, lean, JIT, cycle time, and other management philosophies.

Boeing Lean

System sourcing is a strategy where one supplier provides a major assembly as opposed to many smaller suppliers providing subassemblies or even components. For example, the Boeing Commercial Airplane group in Seattle previously produced the door liner for the Boeing 777 airplane in-house. The bill of materials for the end item consisted of more than 150 part numbers from more than 50 suppliers. The parts were ordered from different suppliers and were delivered to the Boeing 777 production line to meet Boeing's final assembly schedule. This was complicated and caused plenty of variation for Boeing.

Lean management attempts to eliminate unnecessary variation. Boeing wanted to become lean by reducing the number of production parts suppliers. How was this done? Now, a systems supplier provides the final subassembly of the door liners. Once the final subassembly is

CONTEXT: Lockheed Principles of Lean Manufacturing

- **Visual transparency.** If you can't see it, you can't manage it. Visual management implies there is a clear display of charts, list and records of performance problems.
- **Design For Manufacturing and Assembly.** DFM/A ensures products can be produced easily and consistently with high value add.
- **Process focus.** Process focus is the essential element of all supply chain, improvement, six sigma, and lean manufacturing initiatives. The supply chain looks at the overall process, while lean manufacturing looks at maximizing subprocesses, production cells, and machines. Each discrete operation is analyzed and stabilized before the entire process chain can be stabilized. The end result is a streamlined flow of products.
- **Just in time.** In a JIT, pull system, specific products are produced as they are needed, when they are needed and only in the quantity they are needed. Constraints or stress on the weak supply chain links will be quickly uncovered or discovered.
- **Process control.** Process control ensures that unusual process conditions can be detected quickly, corrected, and prevented from recurring.
- **Standard work.** Fundamental to all lean is that repetitive activities should be standardized and proceduralized. This means that work steps are flowcharted and procedures are written capturing best practices and lessons learned. This way if critical people leave, core processes are still stable.[10]

completed, the designated supplier delivers the door liner just in time to be fit on the 777.[9] Under this approach, everyone wins. Boeing shifts responsibility for the subassembly, quality, and delivery to the supplier. The Boeing 777 production line has fewer parts to worry about.

The benefits realized by Boeing under this strategy included less variation in a number of areas specifically:

- Simplified bills of material.

CONTEXT: Lean Work Tips

- Work with selected supply-partners to help them develop lean processes.
- Level production schedules to avoid big spikes in demand, which allow suppliers to minimize inventories.
- Create a disciplined system of delivery time periods when parts shipments have to be delivered.
- Develop lean transportation systems to handle mixed load, small lot deliveries.
- Encourage suppliers to ship what are needed to the assembly plant at a particular time.[11]

- Reduced legal and contracting costs.

- Reduced number of suppliers.

- Reduced assembly costs.

- Reduced travel time and expenses by eliminating travel to numerous suppliers.

- Reduced nonconformances.

- Reduced cycle time.

Daimler Benz Lean

Mercedes-Benz assembles its M-Class sports utility vehicle at the Vance, Alabama plant. The plant has adopted a strategy in which a single supplier provides entire systems on a JIT basis. For example, instead of buying head rests and seat cushions from different suppliers for subassembly in-house, Mercedes receives fully assembled seats from a designated supplier.

There are more than 200 deliveries a day to the Alabama plant, from more than 65 sources. Suppliers are required to sequence their deliveries so they arrive at the plant in the proper order for daily production.

Johnson Controls Lean

In many ways, lean management is just in time management. For example, lean delivery involves a just in time relationship with suppliers. In one case, Toyota formed a close partnership with Johnson Controls to deliver seats to be just in time installed on the assembly line. Inventory levels dropped form 32 days of inventory to 4.1 days. Along with this, set up times for dies and machinery were reduced from hours to as little as 17 minutes.[12]

QUALITY MANAGEMENT

One consequence of postwar technology has been the acceleration of change in our society, so that we seem to produce a new generation of products about every five years.
Ross Macdonald

High quality products and services are essential to supply chain management. If a supplier produces nonconforming products, these rejected products cause production lines to stall unless there is some buffer inventory.

Today's approach to quality is called six sigma. Six sigma companies call it a philosophy, a set of guiding principles as well as a set of tools. Regardless of the term, six sigma is a widespread method for improving production quality and delivery of goods and services.

THE SIX SIGMA QUALITY REVOLUTION

Quality like purchasing has gone through several changes. Quality management has been called process improvement, quality control, total quality management, business process improvement, and now six sigma. Are all of these the same? No. However, the intent is the same, which is to satisfy customers with improving products delivered on time and on budget. More often, the intent is to exceed customer expectations with improved products and services. In commercial and industrial purchasing, the supply manager is the customer who wants products delivered in sequence in tighter time windows while lowering overall costs.

CONTEXT: The Motorola Story

Motorola is among the first companies to promote six sigma techniques. Now Motorola and others use these systems to drive higher levels of improvement with suppliers. Motorola expects verifiable improvement in four critical areas:

- Keeping pace in attaining perfect product quality.
- Remaining on the leading edge of product and process technology.
- Practicing just-in-time manufacturing and delivery.
- Offering cost-competitive service. [14]

Six sigma has almost become a cult of perfectibility. GE's CEO Jack Welch single-handed launched six sigma. Before that, it was a techie statistical tool for improving a process. Welch needed a measurable methodology to baseline and benchmark business performance. Six sigma fit the bill perfectly. All of a sudden, it became an enterprise improvement ethic. And it worked. According to GE, six sigma added $600 million to GE's bottom line in one year alone.[13]

PARTS PER MILLION QUALITY LEVELS

Companies in competitive environments expect parts per million (PPM) quality levels from suppliers. Historically, firms purchased parts according to acceptable quality level (AQL) criteria. Using AQLs, companies usually accepted products with 1,000 or 10,000 parts per million defect levels.

SCM processes require very high consistency and high quality levels. Six-sigma quality by definition is 3.4 parts per million defect levels. Very high quality? You bet. Thousands of US companies are pursuing six sigma. Fad du jour? Maybe! The reality is that most US companies still have quality levels around 3000 parts per million.

CONTEXT: Mikel Harry's Six Sigma Methodology

Measure
1. Select CTQ (critical to quality) characteristic.
2. Define performance standards.
3. Validate measurement system.

Analyze
4. Establish product capability.
5. Define performance objectives.
6. Identify variation sources.

Improve
7. Screen potential causes.
8. Discover variable relationships.
9. Establish operating tolerances.

Control
10. Validate measurement system.
11. Determine process capability.
12. Implement process controls.[15]

FINAL PRODUCT QUALITY IS ONLY AS RELIABLE AS THE COMPONENTS

A finished product is only as reliable as its smallest component. Since a finished product is the sum of many small parts, which form a subassembly, assembly, and finally, a finished product, the smallest component can cause the whole unit to fail. For example, if a tiny rivet on an aircraft bulkhead fails, there can be a cascading effect where the pressurized bulkhead buckles and causes the pilot to lose control of the aircraft. If a manufacturer obtains many small components from suppliers, each component has to be as robust and reliable as the finished product.

In electronics, parts per thousand defect rates especially can't be tolerated. For example, many electronic components are wired in series. If one series component fails then the whole component can fail. In a hypothetical computer that had 10 printed circuits boards each containing 10 components, if the parts were 1% defective, then as many as 97% of the computers would end up with at least one defective part. Depending on the wiring configuration, one defective component could create a malfunction making the whole computer inoperable. The solution: electronic supply managers are requiring suppliers to ship parts with no more than 10 parts per million defect rates.

WHY DOES SIX SIGMA QUALITY WORK?

Why has six sigma worked when other quality initiatives have stalled? There are a number of reasons. Six sigma is often a top down initiative which senior management actively supports. Employees get trained in problem solving as 'project champions' or as 'black belts.'

Six sigma projects are usually doable, measurable and manageable. This ensures demonstrable business results. While results can vary, improvements of $50K to $250K in cost savings or cash generating impacts are often common.

BENCHMARKING MANAGEMENT

If we have had a formula for growth it has been; start with the best; learn from the best, expand slowly and solidify our position; then horizontally diversify our expertise.
Mark McCormack, writer

Benchmarking is a critical method for measuring supply management improvement. Benchmarking is the continuous process of comparing and measuring processes, systems, services, practices, and products against leading companies inside or outside one's industry sector.

'BEST IN CLASS'

Benchmarking has been around for about 20 years. It is pretty simple. It looks at who's doing what, usually called best practices and then compares these against what is done internally. A gap analysis then reveals what best practices can be integrated internally or with suppliers.

Often a benchmarking study is the impetus for a company to discover that something is wrong and the solution is to adopt supply chain management. The competition is doing something critical in half the time and is reaping tremendous profits from this strategy. Evaluating and if necessary redesigning internal supply chain processes is the first step to increasing time-to-market. First a company eliminates wasteful or nonproductive internal tasks and then external supply chain processes are targeted for similar improvement.

Companies can benchmark just about any activity. For example, the following SCM practices can be benchmarked: electronic data interchange (EDI), supply certification, quality practices, project delivery, commodity costs, manufacturing resource planning (MRP), JIT delivery, and customer-supply partnering.

TYPES OF BENCHMARKING PROJECTS

There are 4 basic types of benchmarking projects: 1. internal, 2. competitive, 3. functional, or 4. generic benchmarking.[16] Often, benchmarking companies look for tips outside an industry sector because it is easier to gather information. These companies aren't paranoid about a competitor stealing a secret and are more willing to share information.

Benchmarking may be a one-time effort or it may be a continuous process of comparing a company's supply chain against a competitor's. Companies that continuously benchmark learn to adapt and adopt new practices quickly. It is critical that benchmarking companies look for companies that have 'world class' processes. A benchmarking project as any related SCM initiative should reinforce the organization's strategic vision and mission.

Unfortunately, the above requirements are not always followed. The scope of the SCM benchmarking project may be too broad and not easily achievable. For example, a study to benchmark the best practices of a wafer fab operation is difficult if not impossible. These plants may cost a billion dollars. They have state-of-the-art technologies that companies don't want to share with competitors.

In general, benchmarking offers the following benefits:

- Establishes achievable improvement targets.

- Breaks down the 'why break it if it works' thinking.

- Destroys preconceptions.

- Initiates an organizational and supply chain cultural change.

- Establishes a SCM improvement methodology.

- Sets accountabilities for supply process and product improvement.

HOW TO BENCHMARK

Robert C. Camp, the author of the best selling **Benchmarking**, outlined the following steps of a successful benchmarking project:

- **Identify what is to be benchmarked.** Define the mission, deliverables, and performance measurements of the SCM benchmarking project. Understand the SCM process, product, or procedure to be benchmarked.

- **Identify comparative supply chains.** Identify the best competitors or industry leaders from whom supply chain lessons can be learned. As well, determine the appropriate form of benchmarking, i.e. competitive, internal, functional, or generic benchmarking. Approach selected companies to be benchmarked and have backup companies. Identify constraints to benchmarking within or outside one's industry.

- **Determine a data collection method and then collect the data.** Determine how information is to be gathered. Information can be collected from internal sources such as internal experts or through public domain information such as external experts and consultants.

- **Determine current performance 'gap'.** Gap analysis investigates differences in present practices, performance, cost, quality, or efficiency against those that were benchmarked.

- **Project future performance levels.** Is the gap widening or closing and at what rate? This analysis provides understanding of the gap and what can be done to close it by deploying new practices or procedures.

- **Communicate benchmark findings and gain acceptance.** The results of the benchmarking study have to be communicated to the appropriate stakeholders by providing specific recommended actions.

- **Establish functional goals.** Benchmarking results are then operationalized, translated into functional, attainable goals.

- **Develop action plans.** The actions to achieve functional plans and goals may involve implementing process controls, establishing process capability, developing new training methods, or pursuing other system/process improvements.

- **Implement specific actions and monitor progress.** Specific actions are implemented to achieve goals. Implementation can be through line management or supply management. Progress is then continuously monitored.

- **Recalibrate benchmarks.** Progress reports determine if benchmarked practices are being implemented according to plan. If not, the process is corrected or recalibrated.[17]

CONTEXT: Benchmarking Warning Signs

- Lack of senior management sponsorship.
- Wrong people on the benchmarking team.
- Lack of true understanding of how target companies implemented practices.
- Unmanageable benchmarking team.
- Underestimation of time, resources, and efforts required to complete and implement benchmarking results.
- Over emphasis on reaching performance targets instead of focusing on improvement processes.
- Use of benchmarking as a tool, instead of a positioning strategy.
- Use of benchmarking for minor challenges instead of furthering strategic objectives.
- Too many site visits especially when information can be researched or is a phone call away.
- Failure to follow up on benchmarking implementation.[18]

LOGISTICS MANAGEMENT

The telephone book is full of facts, but it doesn't contain a single idea.
Mortimer Adler

Logistics is the movement of goods and parts within the supply chain. Traditionally, logistics was a weak link in the chain because truck, plane, and ocean carriers couldn't identify and locate goods. Suppliers would carry buffer or safety inventory so a missed or delayed shipment would not stop production. Well, technology has made this much easier.

WHAT IS LOGISTICS MANAGEMENT?

Logistics, simply defined, is a set of practices to determine how to move people and materials most efficiently between a given source and destination. The 'supply chain' metaphor further extends this idea to denote a group of loosely connected companies, all collaborating on the efficient and economic delivery of products.[19]

APICS has a more formal definition of a logistics system:

> "The planning and coordination of the physical movement aspects of a firm's operations, such that the flow of raw materials, parts, and finished goods is achieved in a manner that minimizes total costs for the levels of service desired."[20]

The critical point is that a supply chain is only as good as its product delivery system. The movement, preservation, packaging, and inventorying of products are managed throughout the supply process from critical supply-partners to users. Again, the goal is to reduce variation and ensure consistency. Full truckloads of the correct materials packaged suitably are sent to the right location, in the right sequence for unloading at the right time. Less than truckload costs are also managed. Truckload times are reduced. Products are bar coded. Product counts and inspection are eliminated entirely.

Logistics management has many common elements with just in time management. For example, critical elements of logistics management include:

- **Elimination of incoming receiving inspection.** Inspection is entirely eliminated. The quality engineer may receive an incoming statistical process control (SPC) chart indicating incoming products were process-controlled. Quality engineers develop quality standards to which the suppliers must demonstrate compliance.

- **Direct logistics.** Materials come directly from the supplier. Repeated transferring among different transporters is eliminated thereby reducing transportation damage.

- **Accurate counts.** Quantities delivered to the customer are exact. Shipments are delivered on an as-required basis. There is no permanent incoming or buffer inventory. Material arrives just in time to be used.

LOGISTICS MANAGEMENT

Trucks, trains, ships, and planes carry products. The mode of transportation is determined by the value of the goods, cost of transportation, and demand for the products. The supply manager often determines the best method of transport.

As cycle times shrink and demand for goods changes, supply managers find their work is becoming more difficult. Manufacturers won't stockpile parts wanting them just in time for use. So, the responsibility for balancing transport flow and ensuring timely delivery falls on the supply manager or a logistics person.

To ensure JIT delivery, supply managers and logistics experts want just in time status information of the shipment. How is this done? The buyer and carrier are electronically linked. The carrier has a wide array of technologies that can be used. Shipments and products may be bar coded and assigned to a specific carrier. Carriers then monitor the shipment using satellite-tracking technology.

SUMMARY

SCM labels can be damaging. Let's look at a few. If we now need to be lean, what were we before, fat and lazy? If we need to do six-sigma quality, what were we before, shoddy and sloppy? If we're going to do just in time, were we doing just late?

Supply chain management is based on simple management truisms, such as being lean, reducing variability, managing by exception, and managing using the Pareto Principle. Lean implies cutting all fat from all processes. Supply stream implies the entire production or service chain is smooth. While the techniques discussed in this chapter are obvious, they are not consistently applied. Why? They take energy, daily commitment and challenge the ways people work

Do all of these tools and techniques work well? Frankly, organizations must tailor them and even then there are challenges.

CHAPTER 8:
SCM PROCESS MATURITY MODELS

The term 'quality' has disappeared from much of the supply chain management literature. However, the concept of quality as process management and control is thoroughly embedded in supply chain thinking and doing. All mature supply chain initiatives employ lean, just in time, demand-pull, six sigma, quality function deployment, lifecycle costing, design for manufacturability and other mature process concepts. In this chapter, we'll introduce the process maturity concept and apply it to supply chain management.

SUPPLY MANAGEMENT IS PROCESS MANAGEMENT

Reorganization is the permanent condition of a vigorous organization.
Roy Ash

Supply chain management is fundamentally supply process management. In other words, all supply streams and chains are process flows. Examples of SCM process flows include: information management, product development, production flow, and product delivery.

A full supply chain can be massive involving many thousands of suppliers throughout the world. So when people refer to a supply chain, it is critical to scope what is meant by the concept. Are we talking about first-tier suppliers including their suppliers (2nd tier and lower)? If we are, the magnitude of the supply chain becomes huge and unmanageable. For the sake of this chapter's SCM discussion, the 'critical few' suppliers are first-tier or key supply-partners.

END-TO-END SUPPLY CHAIN CAPABILITY AND MATURITY

The supply management process system starts and ends with the customer. It starts by identifying customer needs, wants, and expectations. It ends by producing a product or delivering a service that satisfies or exceeds these needs, wants, and expectations.

Each process step from marketing to shipping a finished product must value. Marketing determines what customers' needs are and communicates these to the organization. Engineering designs a product to customer requirements. Supply management then buys components and parts to be machined or assembled into a finished product. Suppliers provide various types of products. Manufacturing produces the product. Distribution delivers it to the customer. Quality monitors conformance throughout the process. This pattern is repeated each time a new product is developed or an existing product is modified.

Each critical step must demonstrate process control and capability. Control is the ability to be stable and consistent around a performance target. Capability is the ability to meet a standard or specification consistently.

MATURITY AND CAPABILITY

Everything is connected to everything else.
Barry Commoner

A recurring theme in this book is that supply management's role is changing from procuring products at the lowest price to securing reliable supply processes. This move from a low price, product focus to a process emphasis is a paradigm shift. How does supply management manage the product to process shift? Suppliers are asked or required to move up a customer-supply capability and maturity curve (see figure on the next page.)

```
              ┌──────────────────────────────────────────┐
              │                                            │
              │                    Supplier Partner        │
              │         ▲                          ┌─────   │
              │ Quality/│                          │        │
              │ Cost/   │                          │        │
              │ Delivery/│       Preferred Supplier│        │
              │ Tech    │                   ┌──────┘        │
              │ Level   │                   │               │
              │         │                   │               │
              │         │ Approved Supplier │               │
              │         │            ┌──────┘               │
              │         │            │                      │
              │         │            │                      │
              │         │            │  Candidate Supplier  │
              │         └────────────┴──────────────────▶   │
              │                                            │
              │                    TIME                    │
              │                                            │
              │   Customer-Supply Capability and Maturity Curve │
              └──────────────────────────────────────────┘
```

Customer-Supply Capability and Maturity Curve

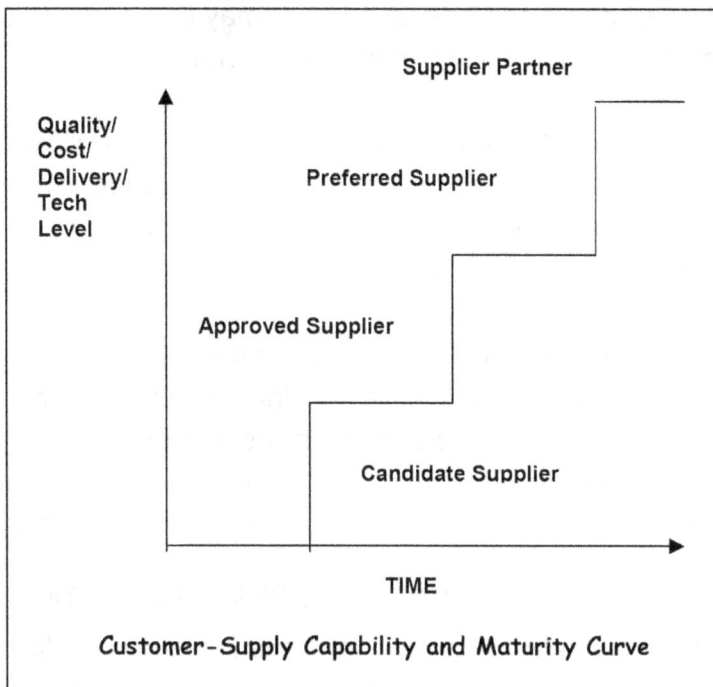

CUSTOMER-SUPPLY MATURITY

Supply management is responsible for assuring that supply quality, technology, delivery, cost, and service processes can meet customer requirements and can complement internal core capabilities. This is the main reason why supply management is being elevated to the chief purchasing officer (CPO) level. This is critical to all organizations that spend a large part of their manufacturing dollar buying products and services from suppliers.

What's the best method of assuring high quality, low cost products? Today's best SCM practice is to partner, develop, and integrate a critical few suppliers into a seamless process chain. Suppliers often start as candidate suppliers then move up a maturity curve as their quality, cost, technology, design, delivery, and service process capabilities improve. At each step of the process, supplies are induced, evaluated and measured against demonstrable criteria. This is called supply development. Its critical suppliers are measured in each step of the journey against demonstrable criteria or standards, which may include ISO 9001:2015 or the Baldrige Performance Excellence Program.

Over the lifecycle of the relationship, suppliers mature and grow as supply-partners. Suppliers are expected to continuously improve their quality, cost, technology, and delivery process capabilities so the entire supply chain can maintain a competitive edge.

As SCM increases in importance, more companies want to work with a 'critical few' or 'world class' suppliers. What makes a 'world class supplier?' This supplier has core competencies that the customer doesn't have. In other words, a 'world class' supplier is one with known and demonstrable processes, high on the capability and maturity curve.

MOVING FROM A PRODUCT TO A PROCESS ORIENTATION

The shift from a product focus to a process focus can be illustrated by moving up the supply management maturity and capability curve (see Customer-Supply Capability and Maturity Curve figure). For example, customers will purchase products from a candidate supplier based on acceptable product quality or delivery. These low-level relationships are usually based on low price, anytime delivery, and relatively low quality.

Low level capability and maturity purchasing is often transactional, at one point in time. Transaction relationships are often adversarial, arms-length, win-lose, low price, and short term.

Process based relationships are mutually beneficial, life cycle cost based, and long term. A process orientation implies the supply manager secures the supplier's core process competencies and is aligning these with the customer's core processes thus creating synergies. The process of moving up the curve is called supply development or customer-supply partnering.

SELF MANAGEMENT IS KEY

Supply management looks to suppliers to control and seamlessly integrate their processes into the supply chain. In other words, suppliers are expected to self manage their quality, delivery, and cost processes. This implies there is no incoming material inspection, products are delivered just in time to the proper location, and overall contract cost reductions are shared with the customer.

So, companies increasingly audit suppliers, certify them, and expect zero-defect level performance. If suppliers comply, rewards are shared and they move up the process maturity and capability curve. Suppliers are also induced by larger and longer-term contracts, technical assistance, and special equipment.

FROM PRODUCT INSPECTION TO PROCESS MANAGEMENT

The graveyard of business is littered with companies that failed to recognize the inevitable changes.
Anonymous

Quality, cost, delivery, and technology are the major elements in most industrial and commercial buy decisions. Each element, such as cost or quality, has its own maturity curve. In the supply process chain, quality still reigns as the most important factor in supply selection and development. In this section, we describe the quality capability and maturity journey.

Quality in most organizations matures along this path:

- Inspection.

- Quality control.

- Quality assurance.

- Process management.

INSPECTION

Inspection is product based. The first quality function was an inspection organization whose main responsibility was to direct the work of factory product inspectors. Factory inspectors policed the quality of incoming, in-process, and outgoing products. The department had no independence because it reported to the head of manufacturing.

QUALITY CONTROL

Quality control (QC) was the start of moving from a product to a process based approach to quality where process and product variation was controlled. Why? Stabilized, in control processes produce consistent and conforming products. A department called quality control replaced the inspection department. As the name suggests, prevention through process control was emphasized. Quality control, now independent of manufacturing, monitored manufacturing performance. Quality could no longer be overruled or second-guessed by the department it was supposed to monitor. However, quality control still focused on manufacturing control and didn't monitor engineering design.

QUALITY ASSURANCE

As quality became more important, management realized it needed an independent and objective group to monitor internal quality as well as quality in other functions, such as engineering, supply chain management, and distribution. So, a separate but equal department was created called quality assurance.

The department responsible for quality activities has many titles these days. The department is called quality assurance, quality engineering, or reliability engineering. In the service sector, it is called customer service and customer quality. Regardless of the name, the departments have the same responsibilities, which are to coordinate, maintain, and monitor quality processes throughout the organization and into the supply base.

PROCESS MANAGEMENT

As organizations mature, quality evolves into process management. Quality is prevention oriented and its scope has increased to involve the entire organization and the supply base. At this level, the term 'quality' even disappears and becomes simply excellent management practices.

Responsibility for work rests with the person, work unit, or supplier performing the work. At the simplest level, this may be a person on the line or a person who delivers products to the customer. Only this person can add or degrade product or service value.

Continuous supply process improvement is also key to the supplier's suppliers, second-tier and lower. Process improvement or simply business management can involve a number of activities including standardizing processes, decreasing process variation at required targets, improving time-to-market, becoming lean, increasing customer satisfaction, or improving process capability.

PROCESS MATURITY AND CAPABILITY MODELS

No progress is going back.
Proverb

For years, U.S. companies dominated world markets by being vertically integrated. In **Purchasing Strategies for Total Quality**, I wrote,

> "Conventional wisdom said that if a company owned the sources of raw material, processed the raw material, designed the products, machined, fabricated, marketed, and finally distributed the products, products and market share would be assured. Vertical integration offered the advantages of standardization of products; control of operating, marketing, and distribution channels; and size and cost efficiencies."[1]

This could be seen in the auto industry where automakers controlled the entire design, manufacturing, and distribution and marketing chain. Little was purchased and almost everything related to developing an automobile was performed in-house. It was believed that if a company owned the sources of raw materials, designed the product and controlled the mechanisms for selling distributing, and servicing the product, the company could control product delivery, quality, service, and costs.

PROCESS BASED, BUSINESS MODELS

Now, most business models are core process based. Why? In today's global economy, individual customers want customized products and services, not me-too global products. Thus, we see the rise of mass customization strategies to satisfy different customers based on a standard product chassis and customized peripheral elements, such as product color. To produce and sell products in small quantities in niched markets requires integrated supply chain processes.

In the last few years, we've seen the development of proprietary supply process models and maturity models.

KPMG BUSINESS MODEL

Based on the premise that information is power, KPMG has developed a 'fragmented pyramid' based on a virtual supply chain model consisting of 5 levels:

- **Stage 1 - The Fragmented Pyramid.** At this stage, distinct functions such as R&D, manufacturing, and transportation share information electronically. But, accounting, sales and warehousing probably aren't. The company isn't well connected with suppliers.

- **Stage 2 - The Process Pyramid.** At this stage, the company is starting to integrate its departments along process lines, but isn't linked with its suppliers or customers. It's starting to think about doing so, which is a crucial first step.

- **Stage 3 - Integrated Principles.** The company has integrated all its internal business processes. Often, larger and dominant companies can require supply integration and can demand buying information.

- **Stage 4 - Enterprise to Enterprise.** The company can share real time information time with suppliers and has linked planning and forecasting systems.

CONTEXT: Mature Supply Chain Practices

- Predictive or preventive maintenance.
- JIT/continuous-flow production.
- Focused-factory production systems.
- Quick-changeover techniques.
- Bottleneck/constraint removal.
- Cellular manufacturing.
- Pull system/kanbans.
- Lot-size reductions.
- Competitive benchmarking.[3]

- **Stage 5 - Virtual Network.** In the final stage, the company is connected with its trading partners in a number of ways, essentially creating a virtual 'trading community.'[2]

AUTO INDUSTRY CAPABILITY MODEL

During the 1990's, high tech companies, aerospace, and automakers entrusted suppliers with developing and providing larger assemblies of products. To reduce costs and improve delivery, more automakers require first-tier suppliers to build entire systems, modules, or assemblies instead of just supplying parts and components. These suppliers are called system integrators. System integration follows three maturity levels.

- **Level 1. System is assembled by the supplier.** Component parts, cost responsibility, and product development responsibility remains with the original equipment manufacturer (OEM).

- **Level 2. OEM retains control of suppliers and sets cost.** The OEM does product development, but tier one suppliers take responsibility for quality assurance and parts ordering.

- **Level 3. Full turnkey.** The tier-one supplier assembles a system of products and has full sourcing and product development responsibilities for that assembly.[4]

SUPPLY CHAIN COUNCIL'S MATURITY MODEL

The Supply Chain Council's model identified four supply chain processes: areas: plan, source, make, and deliver. Companies study their process flows and match them against the Supply Council's benchmarked data.

The Council's framework consists of four levels:

- **Level 1** broadly defines the key supply chain processes - plan, source, make, and deliver - which companies can use to develop their SCM objectives.

- **Level 2** defines 26 core process categories that can be found in an idealized supply chain. For example, the 'source' category includes 'sourced purchased materials,' 'sourced engineer-to-order products,' and 'sourced make-to-order products.'

- **Level 3** has benchmarked information for companies to plan and tailor their SCM strategies, using process definitions, 'best in class' benchmarks, and software capabilities.

- **Level 4** focuses on implementation. Because SCM implementation is unique to each company, Level 4 elements are not specifically defined.[5]

'PULL OR PUSH' PROCESSES

Do you push or pull a chain?
Anonymous

As companies move up the maturity and capability curve, supply managers want seamless, and integrated processes from supply-partners.

CONTEXT: Supply Chain Tips and Tools

- Plan and deploy inventory effectively.
- Provide predictable delivery performance.
- Create new products and services.
- Reduce order fulfillment cycle time.
- Reduce products in stock.
- Decrease manufacturing cycle times.
- Reduce transportation costs.
- Reduce customer returns.
- Communicate electronically with customers and suppliers.[6]

So when there is customer order, the tailored product can be made to the customer's requirements.

PUSH PROCESSES

For a supply chain to work smoothly, there should be a realistic estimate of product demand. Products flow through supply processes. There are two types of flows: push and pull. And, there are various combinations between these two.

Traditional batch manufacturing follows a push model. Push demand starts from sales estimates, an estimate of how many products will be purchased, which determine how many products will be produced. If the push forecast is too high, then extra products go into inventory. If the push forecast is too low, then extra shifts may be required to produce the required number of products. Whatever happens, if the projections are too high or too low, there is a ripple or 'bullwhip' effect down and up the supply chain? Specifically, bottlenecks or high inventory arise.

PULL PROCESSES

Pull demand systems are fundamentally just in time and 'build to order' (BTO) processes. Customers create the demand, which may be retail or user consumption. This information flows up the supply chain to create the demand for additional products to flow down the chain. In a pull system, the customer defines what products are required and this determines product demand.

Build-to-order business (BTO) is a popular pull model and is used by many companies to reduce inventories. Dell early on saw the opportunities and patented many elements of its BTO business model. Amazon.com is also famous for its patented 'one-click' model – one mouse click ensures the on-line order. The unqualified success of companies such as Dell Computer, Amazon.com, and Cisco Systems, which carry little inventory and use their supply management expertise as a competitive advantage, has driven many supply chain manufacturers to BTO pull systems.[7]

What's a better process, push or pull? This question has huge impacts and helps frame the supply chain management discussion. Let's go back to the supply chain metaphor. It is powerful and simple. Do you push or pull a chain? We're hearing more about 'demand chain' processes. The visual has some appealing qualities. It tells the world how the supply chain works. It implies every part of the chain is customer sensitive. And, the supply management function has a key element to manage the process.[8]

THE POWER OF INFORMATION TECHNOLOGY

Technology has greatly increased the accuracy of estimating and predicting customer demand. Let's look at how information technology helps estimate demand in retail businesses. The traditional method of determining retail demand is the open shelf ordering process. The order clerk checks daily or weekly how many products have been sold and fills open shelves with inventory from the back room. If the order clerk over-projects demand in one store, then there is high inventory. If done in hundreds of stores, this can be catastrophic in the high volume, low margin retail business. If order clerks underestimate demand, then there are lost sales and unhappy customers.

One solution is to pull products through production based on real customer orders. There are a number of benefits of doing this. Suppliers can produce products in small batches. Products move quickly through the supplier's plant. There is a daily movement of products from the store to the consumer, from the manufacturer to the store, from the supplier to manufacturers and so on up the supply stream.

In many retail supply chains, product sales are electronically monitored and communicated to the respective suppliers. Consumer purchases generate demand information so products flow to where they are needed. This 'build to replenishment' business model works as long as information is transmitted real time to the distribution center, prime manufacturer and suppliers. Immediate order forecasts can be developed with high accuracy and reliability. These serve as the basis for longer-range forecasts for product delivery and new product introductions months into the future. Again, this works fairly well if there are stable market and demand conditions.

KEEP CUSTOMERS HAPPY

Bad things can happen to great supply chains. There can be poor replenishment of hot selling products. 'Out of stock' stickers make unhappy customers. Excessive inventories are expensive for everyone in the supply chain.

In a pure just in time system, there is no inventory. But, the reality is that the cost of a process hiccup, whether it is a partial delivery, lost shipment, or production slowdown can infect the entire supply chain and result in dissatisfied customers. All of which are costly. So, the supply manager and stakeholders must make a risk analysis and determine the probability of such an occurrence. If a partial or no delivery is unacceptable, then buffer inventory must be used to manage and smooth out the production flow and supply stream.

MANAGING THE 'BULLWHIP'

In a multiproduct, production environment, uneven demand and no buffer inventory make it even more difficult to keep a supply chain running smoothly and to keep the supply links coordinated. If the process isn't managed carefully, there is a bullwhip effect where production lots increase, transportation/logistics is disrupted, and inevitably customers don't get products. In the bullwhip effect, even small changes in a schedule at the customer's plant can lead to disruptions up and down the supply chain.

How can the supply stream deal with the bull whip effect? Demand can be leveled by selective buffer inventories at critical links of the supply chain.

This is a supply chain and lean management reality. Lean, just in time and other optimal supply techniques only work well when there is a steady demand stream of products. When spikes or troughs arise in supply or demand then the buffer inventories take up the slack.

Supply chain spikes or troughs in demand are real supply chain head-aches. The only way to lessen their impacts is to manage inventories. Who has the inventory and who pays for it can become a shell game. Inventory can be found at the supplier's facility, in transit, in a ware-house, at a distributor, or at a number of areas in the customer's facility.

INVENTORY MANAGEMENT

Another method to ensure sufficient parts are available at critical points of the supply chain is to push inventory requirements onto suppliers. This is called supply inventory management. Of course, this is planned and negotiated between the customer and supplier. Jointly managing parts and inventory helps both parties establish their own production schedules and requirements.

Who pays for this inventory is a critical question. The inventory may be collocated with the supplier and the customer. Or, the supplier may carry most or all the inventory. This only works if there is mutual trust for absorbing and allocating costs. Inventory management isn't the best answer to the perfectly lean supply chain. But sometimes, it is the opti-mal response for keeping the chain running smoothly.

SUMMARY

Supply chain management sounds great and looks easy on paper. However, it is extremely difficult. There is no set of rules for successful supply chain management. For example, just in time, demand-pull production makes sense for all parties. However, delivery and production curtailment risks are real in tightly integrated BTO supply chains. One hiccup, labor dispute, broken down truck, and process stoppage can result in no stock. The manufacturer's production line stops, albeit for a short time.

Many factors have to be balanced to keep a supply chain running smoothly, keeping utilization rates high, and reducing inventories, especially when the corporate mandate is to keep the final customer always satisfied.

The politics of 'always satisfy the customer' and 'use the best SCM management tools' can also conflict. What does a supply manager do if there is a corporate mandate: 'never stock out of a product.' The company may need the product to mitigate health, safety, or environmental risks. Or, the company needs the product for final production. Or, it may be a high margin product. The company doesn't want to lose a single sale or face litigation. Ouch. Well, there has to be some buffer product inventory or approved alternate suppliers somewhere in the supply chain who can supply product on demand. But, these emergency supplied products will come at a premium price.

CHAPTER 9:
SUPPLY DEVELOPMENT PROCESS

The U.K.'s Department of Trade and Industry and other public groups are championing 'partnership sourcing.' This is a global trend as country's are adopting a 'Made in India', 'Made in the UK', and Made in the USA' models.

The Department of Trade said that competitive companies should:

1. Focus on core competencies.

2. Reduce their number of suppliers.

3. Develop strong partnership relationships built on shared information and trust with the remaining suppliers[1].

We've already discussed competitive drivers, the need to focus on core process competencies, and the benefits of outsourcing. In the next few chapters, we discuss how to manage and improve process capabilities through supply development.

SUPPLY DEVELOPMENT PROCESS

Knowledge is power.
Proverb

Supply development is the process of developing customer-supply partnerships. You can think of it as moving up the customer-supply maturity and capability curve that was discussed in the last chapter.

> **CONTEXT: Only As Good as the Weakest Link**
>
> The supply process chain is only as good as its weakest link or weakest supplier. So supply development emphasizes:
>
> - Core processes are flowcharted.
> - Value creation and waste reduction are understood and pursued by critical supply stakeholders.
> - Critical supply chain processes are stable.
> - Critical supply chain processes are capable and improving.
> - Supply chain choke points are identified and eliminated.
> - Information flows quickly to all supply chain stakeholders.
> - Risk points are identified with sufficient controls to minimize risk.

SUPPLY DEVELOPMENT AS CORE PROCESS

A company can't be all things to all people or to all customers. Focusing on core competencies and outsourcing noncore work is the preferred method to be competitive. Large companies also prefer to outsource products to 'world-class' suppliers. What does 'world-class' mean? These suppliers have mature and capable processes to deliver world-class products on time, and to the right location.

Supply development thus becomes the basis of supply integration. Partnering allows a customer to bring key suppliers into the product development process to take advantage of the supplier's core skills, knowledge, tooling and service.

Customer-supply partnering, joint ventures or strategic alliances are also preferred to penetrate new markets, provide a local presence, enhance product quality, lower risk exposures, create a market for new products, establish a local distribution network, resell products, integrate suppliers, and share process innovations.

CUSTOMER-SUPPLY PARTNERSHIPS

The goal of customer-supply partnering is to establish a mutually beneficial long-term alliance or relationship. In some partnering relationships, external suppliers are treated as an extension of the customer. Key suppliers are provided with demand, price, technical, manufacturing, and other sensitive information so a supplier can match processes and capabilities with those of the customer. In these partnering relationships, key external suppliers are treated similarly as internal parts suppliers. External suppliers are monitored and expected to improve at the same rate as internal suppliers. External suppliers are also expected to follow the customer's procedures, adopt similar processes, and establish similar communication protocols.

Customer-supply partnering can take a number of forms. A customer may source to multiple suppliers. Or, a customer may source to a single-source. Or, there are various options in between.

VISUAL METAPHOR FOR PARTNERING

A visual is a powerful metaphor on how things work or how we hope they 'should' work. In customer-supply partnering, all the key players should be on the same side of the table. Opposite side-of-the-table relationships imply self-serving and even adversarial relationships. Same-side-of-the-table relationships are mutually rewarding, long term and trust based. Suppliers are induced not consequenced. Suppliers have the long term win in mind.

Do same-side-of-the-table-relationships work? Yes. The auto and electronics industries have developed long term, close relationships with suppliers. Auto suppliers, in some cases, have been induced to locate their plants as close as possible to the customer's plant so their respective assembly processes can be tightly integrated with frequent deliveries of small lots of parts for just in time assembly.

CONTEXT: Fundamentals of Supply Development

- Understand partnering requirements and expectations.
- Follow a consistent process of selecting, monitoring and improving suppliers.
- Ensure both parties can deliver.
- Understand how fulfilling requirements assists the other party in measurable ways.
- Develop performance, quality, or other metrics for each party.
- Understand today's partners may be tomorrow's competitors.
- Evaluate past performance of partners.
- Evaluate partner's state-of-the-art capabilities.
- Use multidisciplinary, customer-supply teams to improve processes and develop products.
- Use certifications to establish a baseline for supply selection and for benchmarking performance.
- Reduce the supply base, sometimes to single-source partners.

SUPPLIER PARTNERING BENEFITS AND RISKS

The benefits of being a supplier to a large organization are evident. The supplier may secure large contracts, guaranteed margins, manufacturing technologies, special financing, and technical assistance.

For the supplier, there are also partnership risks. A large company may structure its supplier relationships in such a way that key suppliers become captive, in other words the supplier has only one customer. A customer may require high-volume suppliers to modify management and operational processes to comply with its requirements. A large company may require suppliers to invest in additional property, plant, and equipment to increase or to improve production capacity. A company may closely monitor its supply performance and tie future order levels to quality, cost, and delivery targets.

To limit the risk exposure of a single supplier not being able to deliver, supply managers are working with a prime and an acceptable alternate supplier. One supplier gets the lion's share of the business. These two suppliers at the end of the year are objectively evaluated and business is allocated to each depending on the past year's performance.

STARTING SUPPLY DEVELOPMENT

The only management practice that's now constant is the practice of constantly accommodating to change.
William McGowan, MCI Chairman

Where do you start with SCM? There are no hard and fast rules. The SCM journey can be product or supplier specific. For example, high value, high tech suppliers probably would have a different development journey that a threaded fastener supplier or distributor.

However the following are some tips for starting the SCM journey:

SHARE EXPECTATIONS AND INFORMATION

Create a memo of customer-supply understanding. This can be contractual or can be an expectations roadmap. The memo of understanding outlines the expectations and goals of the supply chain or customer-supply relationship. Specific mutual benchmarks as well as milestones and inducements in the journey may be identified for the short, medium and long terms.

Companies may be part of a supply chain and have their own supply chains. It's critical that roles, responsibilities, rules and expectations are developed in a memo of understanding. This will guide SCM behaviors and shape outcomes.

A critical element of the supply chain for critical stakeholders is to build trust and share critical information. Developing mutual trust can be difficult. A company may not want to share proprietary information with the customer and potentially with competitors. Most companies have a proprietary business model or core process that they don't want to share it with potential competitors. Why? A company's core process is what differentiates it from its competition? If all companies had this information, they lose would the value differentiator. Some supply managers

```
┌─────────────────────────────────────────────┐
│ CONTEXT: Supply Managers Want                │
│                                              │
│ •   Improved quality.                        │
│ •   Improved delivery performance.           │
│ •   Understanding of business requirements.  │
│ •   Alternative solutions.                   │
│ •   Help in managing inventories.            │
│ •   Better communications.                   │
│ •   Problems solving.                        │
└─────────────────────────────────────────────┘
```

simply say 'no' to full disclosure even if it's a condition to being fully integrated into the supply chain.

START FIRST INTERNALLY

The SCM journey starts with the first step. It is critical that the journey starts with a critical few suppliers. As situations arise, corrections can be taken to alleviate problems. Lessons learned become institutionalized and can be used to integrate more suppliers into the supply chain.[2]

It is critical to understand and map internal core processes, then move into the supply chain. Processes are mapped or flowcharted so that work can be understood and disconnects identified. This provides problem visibility, provides a sense of process ownership, and encourages cooperation up and down the supply chain.

Flowcharting, planning, and other activities are then moved into the supply stream. A Pareto (80-20) analysis focuses efforts on where they have the most impact. The goal is to communicate mutual wins with suppliers and turn competition into coordination and collaboration. Making this leap requires a great deal of trust and respect among all parties.

Process understanding, implementation, and integration are still the primary challenges for companies starting the SCM journey. SCM is basically process management. The chain is only as strong as the weakest link. So, most SCM initiatives start with building internal process capabilities and then integrating these with suppliers. A customer should be able to say to suppliers: 'do as I do as well as do as I say.'

SELECTING SUPPLIERS

Supplier selection and segmentation has even been called the 'next best practice' in supply management. [3]
Stuart Ian

Best-in-class supply chains select and develop suppliers carefully. They use far fewer suppliers than their competitors and spend less on materials than their industry rivals.

THE SUPPLY CHAIN LIFECYCLE

Supply management follows a cycle that starts with selecting a supplier and continues with supply improvement. The supply development lifecycle usually starts early in the product development cycle and consists of the following:

- Select suppliers.

- Monitor suppliers.

- Improve suppliers.

SUPPLIER SELECTION

In the supplier selection process, supply managers coordinate, and consult with engineering, quality, manufacturing, and other functions to select suppliers. Engineering supplies material specifications. Quality audits supplier's quality systems to ensure the selected supplier can manufacture products that meet specifications. And, manufacturing provides feedback on any changes that may be required of the supplier.

The process of selecting a supplier can be compared to a series of capability hurdles that a supplier must jump over. At each hurdle, the supplier satisfies a customer requirement. A prospective or candidate supplier has to deliver a quality product at a competitive price.

CONTEXT: Tips For Selecting Suppliers

- **Is it critical to the customer?**   What's critical to you, the customer, may not be on the supplier's radar screen. Your concerns, as the customer, should be your supplier's concerns.
- **Is it manageable?**   If you're demanding six sigma quality from the supplier, do you have the time to work with the supplier to monitor and advise them if they have immature processes?
- **Is it measurable?**   There are a lot of low hanging fruit with quick returns in supply development. Focus your attention on these. The Pareto Principle in supply management says that 20% of the supply issues create 80% of the problems. So, start with the 'critical few' supply issues not the 'trivial many.'
- **Can it be done quickly?**   There may be low hanging fruit, but you may need a chain saw to cut the fruit down. This requires you buy a chainsaw and this can be dangerous. Any way you get the idea.

The following are steps in selecting a new supplier:

- Identify candidate suppliers.

- Narrow the supplier list.

- Narrow the supplier list further.

- Select suppliers.

Identify Candidate Suppliers

The first step is to identify prospective suppliers that can manufacture the required products. Suppliers can either be domestic or foreign. A domestic-supplier list can be generated from personal knowledge, industry contacts, catalogs, phone books, trade publications, advertisements, or directories. The foreign supplier list can be generated from chambers of commerce, departments of economic development, U.S. State Department, U.S. Commerce Department, trade representatives, foreign consulates, and trade publications.

Data from these sources is then collected to develop a master list of candidate suppliers. While many U.S. companies prefer to buy American products, a global economy and the need for competitiveness has forced companies to go overseas to obtain the best products at the most competitive price.

Narrow Supplier List

The second step is to evaluate candidate suppliers and to narrow the list to those acceptable to the customer. This is the first cut. Approval depends on factors, such as quality, cost, delivery, technology, and service performance.

Narrow Supplier List Further

The third step is to narrow the supplier list to those capable of manufacturing a product or delivering a service that conforms to specifications. One measure often used in manufacturing is process capability, which refers to the supplier's ability to control a process and consistently meet specifications. Capability implies the supplier has the technical and manufacturing competence to satisfy requirements. Capability is verified through interviews, inspection of product characteristics, review of past manufacturing performance, audit of manufacturing processes, or exchange of product samples.

To evaluate capability, the supplier must have drawings, specifications, standards, and all the relevant information to make a conforming product. Otherwise, the supplier can manufacture a product but not to the quality, performance, or reliability levels required by the customer.

Select Prime Supplier

The last step is to select the prime supplier and maybe an acceptable alternate supplier. As opposed to single sourcing, two sources are sometimes preferred to reduce the risk of receiving unacceptable products and to help ensure future price competition. Supply management coordinates this effort with quality, engineering, manufacturing and other stakeholders. The final decision of selecting the prime supplier rests with the supply manager, because he/she is responsible if contract requirements are not met.

Formal evaluation plans are useful for making the supplier aware of customer requirements and expectations. Details for the evaluation are outlined and then attached to the purchase order.

SUPPLIER SELECTION CRITERIA

Most supply selection uses a 'weighted average method' to evaluate delivery, cost, quality, technology and other performance factors. Each customer factor is given a relative weight according to its importance. For example, quality for high value products would be rated higher than a commodity where cost would probably have a higher rating.

Additional selection criteria may include:

- Supplier performance.

- Location.

- Financial stability.

- Motivation.

Supplier Performance

Supplier performance history reveals if the supplier has been responsive in complying with contractual commitments. If a supplier has a history of satisfactory performance, this provides a degree of assurance that material will be supplied just in time and at the specified quality levels. If the supplier is new, then a reference check of previous customers is essential.

Industrial sourcing decisions, which historically were made based on product price, availability, and service, are also changing. If a supply manager was interested in buying a piece of industrial equipment, he or she first looked at the lowest price when evaluating competitive bids. Sometimes product availability was important if the piece of equipment

---

CONTEXT: What's On The Supply Manager's Mind?

- Quality is the most important factor in supplier selection. On a scale of 1 to 10, with 10 being the highest score, quality issues led all others with a cumulative score of 9.2.
- Delivery continues to lead the list of what supply managers would most like to see suppliers improve and by a margin that is growing from year to year.
- Many companies still don't have a standardized supply-rating system.
- Most supply managers would rather buy from producers than distributors, usually for price reasons, but supply managers report that distributors perform better than producers.
- Most supply managers have outsourced value-added tasks to suppliers and nearly all of them report that suppliers perform these tasks either as well as or better than their own companies.
- Most supply managers have had suppliers involved in mergers/acquisitions, and nearly half say that supply performance has suffered[4]

---

was needed quickly. Service was important if the product was subjected to abuse, prone to failure, or designed to run continuously. Nevertheless, price was the primary consideration when buying a product. This situation has now changed. The primary factor influencing the purchase decision is often 'quality' while other factors may be prominent depending on the type of sourced products or services. While still important, cost, service, and availability are lower priorities.

Location
Location is important because logistical, plant location, just-in-time delivery, or technical assistance requirements mandate the supplier is located near the customer, not half way around the world. If problems arise, they are easier to resolve if the supplier is located down the street.

Financial Stability
Financial stability indicates the supplier has been a going concern for several years. This implies continuity and stability. A customer does not want a supplier of critical components to go bankrupt. A wayward

second-tier supplier providing a critical component can disrupt contractual commitments of the prime contractor and can impact the entire supply chain.

Motivation
Supplier motivation is the supplier's attitude to work with the customer to resolve disputes in a timely and mutually beneficial manner. Disputes in customer-supply relations always arise. If the supplier is motivated, these differences can be resolved quickly and amicably.

CAPTIVE SUPPLIERS
Another supply development strategy is to have a captive supplier. In other words, the customer may or may not have a sole source arrangement with the supplier. But, the supplier has a sole producer arrangement with the customer. The supplier just provides products to customers.

This works for both parties. The customer gets a reliable source for critical products, at a known price, with known technology, with confidentiality, and a full understanding of needs. The supplier gets a long-term contract with known margins. The supplier may also get advice and technical assistance from the customer. This arrangement is probably one of the best ways for a customer to integrate a supplier into the value chain. The customer can apply its process and information capabilities directly with the supplier.

MONITORING SUPPLIERS

Trust, but verify.
President Ronald Reagan

During the selection process and over the contract lifecycle, a supplier is monitored to assure on-going quality, delivery, contractual compliance and improvement.

'WORLD CLASS' SUPPLIERS

Companies want to partner with 'world class' suppliers. What does 'world class' mean to a supply manager? The following are criteria a buyer or customer may look for in a 'world class' supplier:

- ISO 9001:2015 registration.

- Improving quality processes.

- Extensive use of quality metrics.

- Desire to do business on a long-term basis.

- Long term financial stability.

- Advanced material requirement practices.

- Computerized sourcing.

- State of the art facilities.

- Extensive cost controls.

- Advanced QA/QC techniques.

- Research and development.

- Recent investments.

- Management progressiveness.

- Willingness to share costs.

- Product samples.

MONITORING TECHNIQUES

The following are commonly used techniques to monitor a supplier:

- Audits.

- Product samples.

CONTEXT: Honda's Supply Management Process

Supply development requires a trust level that frankly some companies may not want. Japanese transplants are famous for their close customer-supply relationships. Honda of America Manufacturing uses target pricing to identify cost saving opportunities. Honda breaks down cost to the component level and then asks its suppliers to provide a detailed breakdown of their costs, including raw materials, labor, tooling, packaging, deliver and administration. By identifying gaps, between the 'is' cost and 'should be' costs, Honda develops a plan to reduce costs while ensuring the supplier achieves a fair profit.

Honda's purchasing department aggregates the costs and compares them to the target cost. Honda tries not to squander the customer-supply relationship by targeting supplier profits for cost reduction. Sharing confidential information on costing, proprietary processes, and core competitive information can lead to difficulties. This is contentious with many suppliers.[5]

- Process capability analysis.

- Incoming material inspection.

- First-article inspection.

- Certification.

Audits

There are 3 basic types of audits: 1. system, 2. process, and 3. product. A systems audit checks internal documentation for compliance audits. A process audit checks the supplier's cost, quality, delivery, and other critical processes for stability, capability and improvement. A product audit checks the supplied product for conformance to technical standards, performance standards, etc.

A team representing quality, manufacturing, engineering, and supply management may conduct critical supplier audits. Major suppliers are those that provide a large dollar volume of products or supply key

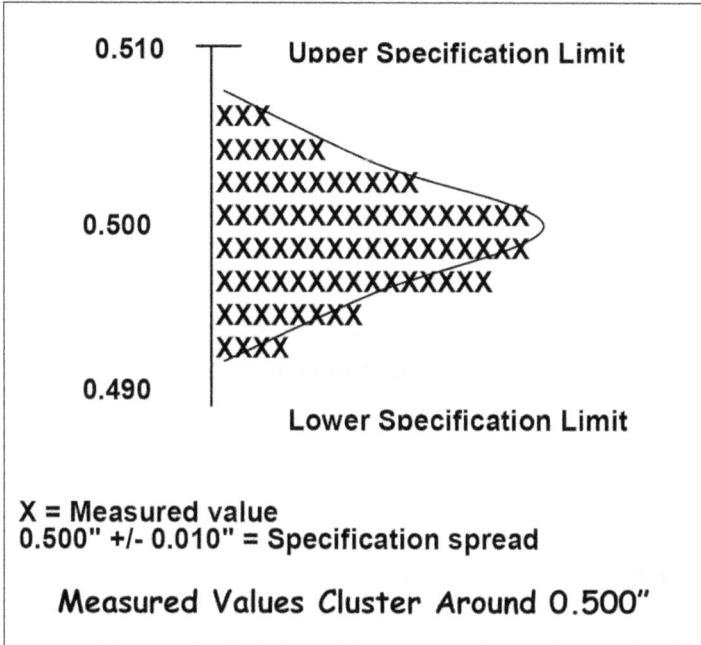

```
0.510  ┬    Upper Specification Limit
          |XXX
          |XXXXXX
          |XXXXXXXXXXX
0.500  |XXXXXXXXXXXXXXXXX
          |XXXXXXXXXXXXXXXX
          |XXXXXXXXXXXXXXX
          |XXXXXXXX
          |XXXX
0.490  |
              Lower Specification Limit
```

X = Measured value
0.500" +/- 0.010" = Specification spread

Measured Values Cluster Around 0.500"

components. A major reason for the adoption of ISO/TS 16949 standards is the ability to check a register of certified suppliers in order to avoid duplicative audits.

Audits are usually formal and highly structured. They begin with an initial discussion about the purpose, scope, and intent of the audit. Depending on the intent and scope of the audit, the following areas can be investigated:

- Quality manual, procedures, and work instructions.

- Organizational structure.

- Logistics processes.

- Cost sharing.

- Technical capabilities.

- Web or business to business capabilities.

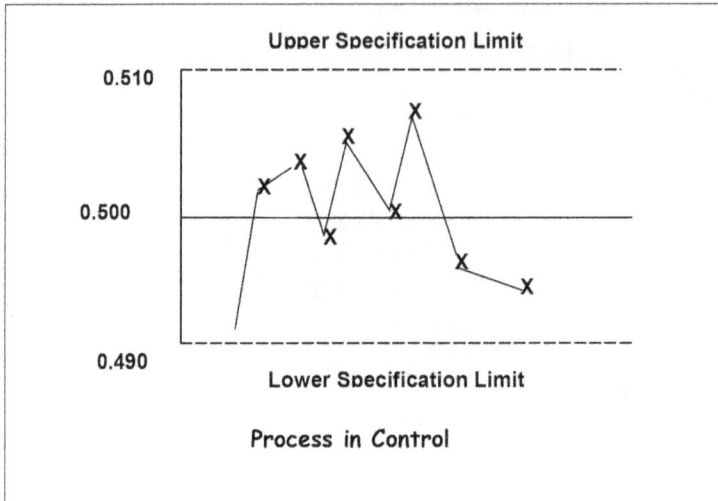

Upper Specification Limit

Process in Control

- Training and certifications.

- Documentation.

- Final product test and evaluation.

- Corrective/prevention actions.

- Measuring equipment and calibration.

- Storage and delivery.

Product Samples
Customers may send a sample product to suppliers when specifications are difficult to develop, such as for products with intricate shapes. Samples are also sent to suppliers to determine if they can be manufactured to specifications and tolerances such as shown in the above figure where the standard value is 0.500 inch and the upper and lower specification limits are respectively 0.510 and 0.490 inches.

Sometimes, parts cannot be specified in writing or depicted in drawings because of intricate geometric shapes. Instead, it is easier to produce a sample product and give this to a supplier to duplicate. The supplier then makes a similar product and submits this to the customer with critical dimensions clearly marked. Then, duplicate measurements using similar instruments are made by both supplier and customer. Appearance, critical measurements, and product performance are verified and any differences are checked. The problem with samples is that product reliability can't be tested. So, a product may conform to all specified measurements but not survive prolonged use.

Process Capability Analysis

Process capability analysis is a statistical study of dimensional variation in a product characteristic (see 'Process in Control' and 'Continuous Improvement' figures). The customer provides the supplier with a small number of parts. Dimensions on parts are measured and compared against the specification. Deviations between the actual measurements and the specifications are analyzed. If measurements are inside and centered in the middle of the specification spread, products are accepted for use. If measurements are outside the specification limits, products are returned to the supplier.

Incoming Material Inspection

Incoming material inspection measures, tests, or checks material from suppliers. Incoming material inspection is time consuming and costly. By checking for nonconformances, the customer is ensuring the quality of the supplier's work. Material is accepted, rejected, or corrected. If accepted, material goes into inventory or directly into production. If rejected, material is used 'as is', reworked, or returned to the supplier.

First Article Inspection

First article inspection is used for inspecting, testing, and measuring the first of a series of products or a significantly modified product that is manufactured by a new or existing supplier. First-article inspection can be a cursory check of critical product or service characteristics or a comprehensive investigation of all physical, functional, and dimensional characteristics of the part or assembly. The degree of the investigation depends on the complexity of the product, the familiarity of the supplier, and time constraints.

CONTEXT: Supply Partnering Benefits and Challenges

Up side:

- High volumes.
- High recognition.
- Preferred access to future projects.
- Improved manufacturing processes.
- Quality gains and lower costs.
- Access to specialized designs.
- Access to production expertise.
- Lower costs.
- Ability to synchronize just-in-time operations.
- Quicker turnaround time.
- Quick change over.
- Fewer problems in design and product change-overs.

Down side:

- Minute scrutinization and operational pressures.
- Customer presence.
- ISO 9001:2015 or other certifications.
- Customer required controls.
- Annual 'report cards'.
- Order levels tied to performance.
- Ever tighter requirements.
- Vulnerability to sharp demand swings.
- Possible loss of other customers.
- Evaluation of past history.
- Assessing security of information.
- Loss of sensitive or proprietary information.
- Loss of customer confidence if failure occurs.
- High opportunity costs.
- Loss of market share.
- Loss of credibility among stakeholders and competitors.
- High entry costs.

First article inspection can:

- Detect early discrepancies, defects, or flaws in the prototype product.

- Serve as proof that specifications can be met.

- Serve as proof that manufacturing set-up is correct.

- Confirm that corrective action modifications have been made.

However, first article inspection can provide misleading results because it:

- Is a snapshot of one item and does not indicate the conformance of the following production products.

- Does not indicate product reliability.

- Does not allow for any process variation that may move dimensions out of the acceptable specification spread.

Certification

Once selected, suppliers are expected to improve product quality, service, delivery, and cost processes. Companies establish formal supplier certification programs to induce suppliers to improve. Suppliers are classified into categories based on process performance, maturity, and capability. Partnering levels include candidate, approved, and preferred suppliers. Or, suppliers may be asked or required to certify to a standard, such as ISO/TS 16949 or ISO 9001:2015.

Supply-partners, the highest certification category, usually have in-house quality, cost, logistical, lean, JIT, or other processes that are equal or more stringent than the customers. Supply-partners are audited periodically to ensure a supplied product is defect-free. Preferred supplier parts are also sent directly into production as part of the lean, just in time production system. ISO 9001:2015 registration is a condition of business for many candidate as well as approved suppliers.

IMPROVING SUPPLIERS

The difficult we do immediately. The impossible takes a little longer.
Anonymous

The traditional purchasing model is the 'across the table', arms-length transactions. There are several problems with this model. Each party distrusts the other. Each party is transaction oriented. Each party tries to maximize the benefits they would receive from the deal.

Each party also works according to its set of preconceptions. The purchaser thinks suppliers will over charge, over promise and under deliver. The supplier thinks that each purchase is the last and will try to maximize the deal. So, buyers play suppliers against each other, switch suppliers on a dime, and offer one time or short-term contracts. The basic business model is short term and adversarial. Supply development and improvement requires a new mindset.

SUPPLIER INDUCEMENTS

Supply chain management is fundamentally a new business model. In other words, core customer and key customer-supply processes must be complementary and must be integrated into a seamless chain. To do this, suppliers must be induced to change, adapt and adopt new practices.

There are a number of simple methods by which to do this. One simple inducement is to ensure that supply-partners are paid in cash with a new purchase order. Lower level suppliers are paid net 30 days.

Being 'designed in' or 'sole sourced' into present or future products can also induce suppliers. The supplier's products are then locked into a long-term contract and the supplier has a greater potential for future business. This type of 'sole sourcing' should be used sparingly because the risks to the customer can be very high.

Other supplier rewards include:

- Longer-term contracts.

- System contracts.

- Technical assistance.

- Public recognition of superior supplier performance.

- New opportunities for business.

- Supplier awards.

- Early involvement opportunities in product development.

KEYS TO LONG TERM RELATIONSHIP

The transactional purchasing model evolves when SCM stakeholders realize that there must be a better way to do business. Adversarial relationships can cause constraints, roadblocks, bottlenecks and lost opportunities. If a supplier has the right attitude and energy, these can make up for other deficiencies. A customer wants to work with a supplier that has the right attitude to improve and collaborate. This applies to first-tier through lower tiers. Supply development often starts with a first-tier supplier.

Joint rules, plans, and forecasts are critical to supply partnering. Real collaboration between companies involves more than sharing information, it is an integrated process that involves joint planning, implementation, and measuring results. The following are critical for maintaining a long-term customer-supply relationship:

- Open and honest communication.

- Trusting relationship.

- Mutually beneficial relationship.

- Continuous improvement.

Open and Honest Communication

The key to maintaining a great customer-supply relationship is open and honest communication that anticipates difficulties and establishes trust. The customer keeps the supplier informed of order changes and design modifications. The supplier keeps the customer informed of changes in delivery dates and production problems. Clear communication settles issues before they become problems or disputes.

Trusting Relationship

Trust is the hopeful outcome of clear communication. If the customer and supplier trust each other, this serves as the basis of a mutually beneficial relationship. The customer consistently receives a defect-free product and knows the supplier will work toward improving product reliability and cost. And the supplier obtains a long-term contract.

In order for SCM to work properly, both customer and supplier must demonstrate:

- Mutual benefits should be real, tangible, and quantifiable.

- Partnership preferably should be based on a formal and binding contract.

- Each party should meet its obligations.

- Continuous improvement of cost, quality, deliver, and service is pursued.[6]

Mutually Beneficial Relationship

The customer tries to establish a mutually beneficial long-term relationship. It is easier to maintain an existing relationship than to start one from scratch. If a supplier has been providing a unique product at a reasonable price with good service, then it makes just good business sense to keep and develop the supplier.

Partners need to share new-product development information. Developing goodwill and trust takes time and effort. Firms can generate trust by exchanging critical technical resources, sharing confidential technology forecasts and drawings, collaborating on strategic plans and long-term product forecasts, or exchanging sensitive financial information.

Continuous Improvement

Suppliers are asked to continuously improve product quality, delivery, and service. In other words, they are asked or required to move up the capability and maturity curve. At a minimum, defect prevention hopes to eliminate routine incoming material inspection. If a supplier can demonstrate a history of defect-free shipments for a period of time, the supplier is audited periodically to ensure internal process controls are followed and documented.

At this point, shipments go directly into production. Supplied product samples may be periodically evaluated or certificates of compliance reviewed. If a number of successive shipments have been accepted and the supplier can prove internal process controls are in place, then a supplier becomes certified and all shipments are sent directly to production. If a shipment is rejected, then shipments are immediately canceled and problems are root-cause resolved.

SUMMARY

In theory, a company should form a strategic supply partnership or alliance when complementary assets can lead to mutual long-term competitive advantages. A customer-supply partnership can be a long-term alliance. Or, it can last to the end of the contract, project, or product lifecycle.

Supply development is the foundation to building a supply chain. The development effort establishes common vision, mission, goals, direction, plans, and benefits with supply-partners. Only then, can disparate supply process stakeholders stabilize processes, ensure capability, and demonstrate long-term improvement. The long-term goal is to form mutually beneficial, long lasting strategic alliances.

CHAPTER 10:
SUPPLY DEVELOPMENT –
CERTIFICATION

Most *Fortune 1000* companies have supply certification programs. Most involve ISO 9001:2015 or industry specific equivalents such as the auto industry ISO/TS 16949. Or, a company may develop its own certification.

Supplier certification was originally conceived and developed as a means to evaluate supply processes and quality systems. ISO/TS 16949 and ISO 9001:2015 are two of the more popular customer-supply certifications. The new ISO 9001:2015 is process based, customer focused and lends itself to SCM.

SUPPLIER CERTIFICATION

If you don't measure it, you can't manage it and it won't happen.
Anonymous

The purpose of supply development is to improve supply quality, delivery, service, cost, and technology processes. Sometimes, specific elements are added that are customer specific.

Increasing a supply-partner's maturity and capability has mutual wins. The supplier gets a heads up on what's coming down the product development pipeline and is in a favorable sourcing position when contracts are bid. Or, the supplier's early involvement can lead to preproduction contracts that can lead to cycle time, cost, and schedule reductions. The customer wins because the company has the benefit of the supplier's core capabilities.

WHAT IS CERTIFICATION?

Supplier certification is a fundamental supply development process. There are several ways to become certified:

- **Self-certification.** A company certifies to the customer that it meets or can meet its requirements.

- **Second-party.** The customer wants a higher level of assurance than self or third party certification. The customer, the second-party, will conduct an on-site system/process/product audit of the supplier's process documentation, which demonstrates compliance to quality, delivery, cost, and technology requirements. The idea is pretty simple. If the supplier's processes are in place according to what documentation says they are, then there is a high level of assurance that the output from the processes, the products, conforms to requirements.

- **Third-party certification.** In the ISO 9001:2015 world, third-party certification is called registration. Registrars will audit companies to ensure they conform to the ISO 9001:2015 requirements. In this way, customers get a level of assurance that the supplier is capable of meeting requirements by checking a registry.

TYPES OF SUPPLIER CERTIFICATION

There are several types of certifications:

- **Product.** Supplied products are tested to verify critical dimensions, performance capabilities, or chemical/physical characteristics. Product testing is often regulatory, ensuring compliance to a standard or regulation. Sometimes, 'first item' testing is the 100% testing or inspection of the first product produced from a process.

- **System.** Systems testing usually deal with policy, procedural, and work instruction conformance. ISO 9001:2015 is one of the best-known system evaluations. System certification is usually binary. Documentation addresses and complies with the standard or it doesn't.

- **Process.** Process evaluations deal with flowcharting a process, following it from beginning to end, checking for risks, and then determining the effectiveness of internal process controls to mitigate risks.

Most supply chain companies conduct systems and product audits but are moving to process assessments.

SUPPLY CERTIFICATION BENEFITS

Let all things be done decently and in order.
Corinthians

Most certification standards focus on core business practices instead of only quality, cost, or delivery requirements. For example, ISO 9001:2015 started as a quality standard and now emphasizes the following:

> "To lead and operate an organization successfully, it is necessary to direct and control it in a systematic and transparent manner. Success can result from implementing and maintaining a management system that is designed to continually improve performance while addressing the needs of interested parties. Managing an organization encompasses quality management amongst other management disciplines."[1]

Supplier certification offers a number of benefits and has become a critical element of supply chain management. Specific benefits include:

- Customer benefits.

- Internal benefits.

- Customer-supply partnering benefits.

CUSTOMER BENEFITS

Supplier certification provides the following customer benefits:

Assists in Developing Products

Time-to-market has become an important driver to SCM success. If supply processes are in control, capable, documented, and improving, a new product can be designed and developed more quickly. Specifically, supplier certification ensures that:

- Supplier organizational structure and quality foundation exist for rapid product development.

- Consistent product development, quality, cost, and delivery language is used throughout the supply chain.

- Core supplier processes are proceduralized.

- Supplier processes are stabilized, capable, and improving.

- Procedures document process standardization and control changes.

Provides Access to Markets

There are a number of accepted certification standards including ISO/TS 16949 in the auto industry and ISO 9001:2015 registration for other companies. Customers want assurance of the supplier's quality capability. Compliance or registration to these standards provides the level of assurance that documentation systems are in place. Thus, products from a Portland, Oregon manufacturer should be consistent with those from a similar Pakistani manufacturer. And, ISO 9001:2015 products should move transparently from one market to another.

Fulfills Contract Requirements

ISO 9001:2015 registration or equivalent compliance to standards appears in more commercial and government contracts largely due to the influence of the auto industry adopting ISO/TS 16949.

Establishes Promotional Credibility

Markets are crowded with competing products and services. Product positioning becomes critically important. 'ISO 9001 registered' often appears in magazine ads and promotions extolling the virtues of a company or product. As well, ISO 9001:2015 registration helps a company stand out and differentiate itself from the competition.

Conveys Operational Integrity and Systems Assurance

ISO 9001:2015 registration conveys to a customer that a supplier, that may be four tiers removed, has established internal quality, design, and other systems that have been audited by an independent and objective third party. In some countries, a company can look up a supplier in an ISO registry and determine if the company is qualified to produce a product.

INTERNAL BENEFITS

Most customer-supply certifications originally focused on quality. Now, they more often emphasize quality improvement, but also cost reduction, on time delivery, and information technology application. The Baldrige Performance Excellence Program is sometimes used as a customer-supply certification and considers many business performance improvement criteria beyond quality.

Internal certification benefits include:

Facilitates Business and Quality Planning

Supply certifications may require identifying stakeholder requirements and developing plans on how these will be satisfied. ISO 9001:2015, for example, requires a company to identify the customer's quality requirements and then internalize these into the organization's design, production, and supply processes.

Is Used to Transform Organizations

American business is undergoing rapid change. A critical ability of a senior manager is to create a sense of urgency, define the direction, and then lead the change. Change goes by different words and may involve supply chain management, lean management, JIT management, or other initiatives. Certifications can be the first milestone in the business improvement journey, which as we discussed follows a process capability and maturity model.

Provides Universal Approach to SCM

Certifications provide a common approach and model for pursuing the SCM journey. They ensure that supply chain stakeholders speak a common language and follow consistent rules. ISO 9001:2015 and Baldrige Performance Excellence Program provide an accepted and universal platform and approach to supply certification.

Can be Used in Many Industries and Organizations

Certification standards are often flexible. Their versatility may be their greatest asset. For example, government agencies, non-profit companies, schools, service organizations, and many other organizations are adopting ISO 9001:2015.

Assists in Establishing Supply Chain Baselines

As emphasized throughout the book, the supply chain is a process or more specifically a series of integrated processes. Certifications can establish a baseline for flowcharting core or risky processes.

Flowcharting and then proceduralizing core supply chain processes offer clear benefits. They detail how critical processes operate. They detail disconnects and allow plans to be developed for connecting disparate processes. Supply processes can then be scrutinized very intensely to determine if they add value.

Provides Insights on Organizational Interrelationships

Certifications often detail and identify requirements for interrelated systems and processes. These are the backbone of a supply chain. When the customer and suppliers can map these, they can identify areas of interaction, constraints, and interrelationships. These can then be leaned.

Encourages Supply Chain Focus

Certifications require policies, procedures, and work instructions are developed and followed. Developing the documentation allows supply process stakeholders to clarify responsibilities, mission, plans, and objectives.

Facilitates Internal Process Control

Management review, internal controls, auditing, closed loop corrective action, and preventive action are the core elements of all certifications. They ensure that processes are in control, are capable, and are improving. If deficiencies arise, they are root-cause corrected. ISO 9001:2015 implementation also establishes the following internal control systems: design control, purchasing control, and document control.

Assists Employees in Understanding and Improving Processes

Properly implemented, certifications encourage supply chain stakeholder 'buy-in.' Stakeholders become engaged in identifying, mapping, proceduralizing, auditing, and correcting process nonconformances.

Encourages Self-Assessment

As mentioned, internal auditing is a major; some would say the most important element of most supply chain certifications. Internal auditing results in the following benefits: processes are continuously monitored; if deficiencies occur, they are root-cause eliminated; and systemic and chronic problems are uncovered.

Maintains Internal Consistency

Process consistency is the hallmark of all supply chains. Unknown or unexpected variation, the opposite of consistency, is the nemesis of all supply chain processes. Stabilized imply delivery consistency, product uniformity, and accurate demand planning.

Ensures Internal Processes Are Lean

Many organizations are on autopilot. They do things because that's the way they've always been done. A certification process forces companies to ask: "What are we doing, do our activities add value to the chain, and can things be done better"? These are all lean questions.

Ensures Product Development and Design Changes Are Controlled

Certifications focus on upstream events as in preventing design non-conformances. Cycle time management and rapid product development are essential for the survival of many companies. Product flaws can result in an expensive recall. The solution is to fix problems at the source, for example in the design stage when the least value has been added to the product. A robust, low cost, high quality product can be designed at this stage. Corrective and preventive systems can be established so deficient products won't end up in the customer's hands. Formal design reviews also minimize after-the-fact design modifications and flaws.

Encourages Customer-supply Problem Solving

Proceduralized operations reveal reengineering and improvement opportunities.

CUSTOMER-SUPPLY PARTNERING BENEFITS

Customer-supply benefits include:

Forms the Basis for Common Partnering Language

More products are outsourced to supply-partners. The goal is to develop aesthetic, safe, reliable, cost-effective products, and services. Certification standards are essentially customer-supply partnering documents. They help to develop a common language between supply managers and suppliers.

Ensures Minimum Level of Quality, Service, and Delivery

Certification standards create a level playing field of suppliers. If certification to a standard such as ISO 9001:2015 is required to be on the approved bidders list, then this implies quality commitment, acceptable level of service systems, and compatible delivery processes.

Facilitates Development of Seamless Supply Chain Processes

More certification standards are becoming process based. Companies are organizing work around integrated processes and systems. The goal is to add value to smooth, seamless processes. As more work is outsourced to capable suppliers, the customer wants to know that their suppliers' processes are stabilized, documented, and are operating properly.

Reduces Supply Base

Variability from required targets is anathema to all supply chain performance metrics. This concept of controlling variation can be applied to many business areas including sourcing. Multiple suppliers of the same product or service can create more variation due to price, delivery, or quality misunderstandings. So, many companies are experimenting with the single source, supplier concept. One key supply-partner provides the product or service instead of two or more.

The supply base of many companies is being reduced through customer-supply certifications. Suppliers are rated as candidate, conditional, approved, or supply-partners. For example, ISO 9001:2015 compliance is often used to satisfy first level certification (candidate) requirements.

Facilitates Just-In-Time Delivery

Customers want the right material delivered just in time, at the proper count, and in the right sequence to the right location. Logistics and product delivery are critical elements of some certifications. For example, ISO/TS 16949 companies must have storage, handling, and delivery processes in place and operating properly, which facilitate just in time delivery. If delivery problems occur, they are resolved quickly.

CONTEXT: Benefits and Disadvantages of Standards

The benefits of standards include:

- Compatibility.
- Interchangeability.
- Intercommunications.
- Trade facilitation.
- Technology transfer.

The disadvantages of standards include:

- Slow to develop.
- Require consensus among many stakeholders.
- Are sometimes obsolete by the time they are published.
- Are often descriptive, instead of prescriptive.
- Don't represent the ideas of all stakeholders.
- Can be difficult to decipher.
- Don't relate to daily business concerns.
- Are difficult to locate.

Assists in Selecting Suppliers

Customers want to partner with 'world class' suppliers. What is world class? Suppliers are evaluated in terms of quality, cost, service, and delivery. Numerical certifications assist in measuring supplier capability and maturity.

Assists in Monitoring Suppliers

Suppliers are periodically assessed for quality, service, delivery, cost, and other factors. Customers within an industry sector will audit suppliers to similar criteria. Multiple audits are costly. Certification compliance or supplier registration avoids redundant audits.

SUPPLY CERTIFICATION STANDARDS

If standards are not formulated systematically at the top, they will be formulated haphazardly and impulsively in the field.
John Biegler

The Baldrige Performance Excellence Program and ISO 9001:2015 are two of the world's most commonly adopted and required standards. ISO 9001:2015 compliance or registration is used as a baseline, threshold certification standard. The Baldrige is used as a benchmark, higher level standard. While they were originally quality standards, they have evolved into business process management documents.

THE BALDRIGE AWARD

The Baldrige recognizes organizations that have implemented 'world class' business systems and processes. The intent of the award is to establish 'world class' performance standards and guidelines.

The Baldrige is the quintessential business award. This characteristic may be its biggest benefit or may even be a liability. The award has been criticized for requiring large expenditures of resources to apply for the award and to prepare for site visits. The other major criticism is that winning the award doesn't guarantee future profits.

A major benefit of the award is that it is a living document. It incorporates the latest in business and process thinking. For example the award in recent years has shifted its emphasis from strategic quality planning to strategic business planning. This change integrates and mainstreams process thinking into a business's strategies, goals, and objectives. Customers use Baldrige criteria as a supply management certification because world-class goals, priorities, and targets are clearly spelled out.

BALDRIGE VALUES AND CONCEPTS

The Baldrige Performance Excellence Program is built upon a set of core values and concepts for ensuring customer satisfaction and improving business performance:

- **Systems perspective.** Systems perspective means managing all parts of organization in an integrated fashion.

- **Visionary leadership.** Senior leadership is focused on ethics, customers, and creating value.

- **Customer-focused excellence.** Customers determine organizational performance and value.

- **Valuing people.** Successful organization values people and its stakeholders.

- **Organizational learning and agility.** Organization focuses on continuous improvement and innovation.

- **Focus on success.** Organization focuses on short and long term success though managing risk.

- **Managing for innovation.** Innovation means creating new products, services, programs, services, processes, and even a new business model.

- **Management by fact.** Management by fact implies that decisions are based on performance measures and facts.

- **Societal responsibility.** Organization stresses public responsibilities including environmental, societal, and health concerns.

- **Ethics and transparency.** Organization stresses ethical beliefs and behaviors including transparency and fairness.

- **Delivering value and results.** Organization focuses on performance results including financial, strategic, leadership, and societal performance.

ISO 9001:2015

Less is more. God is in the details.
Mies van der Rohe

Many companies are developing 'world-class' processes. However, many companies entering a supply chain simply need a basic quality system to prevent deficiencies and to meet customer requirements. ISO 9001:2015 is a well-accepted and basic customer-supply standard. ISO 9001:2015 isn't world-class. It consists of basic quality and business processes such as customer satisfaction, auditing, and design review that are essential elements to supply chain management. A major benefit of using ISO 9001:2015 is that the standard can form the baseline or foundation for continuous improvement of moving up the capability and maturity curve discussed in the last chapter.

ISO 9001:2015 FUNDAMENTALS

ISO 9001:2015 emphasizes seven management principles:

- **Customer focus.** Organizations should meet customer requirements and attempt to exceed customer expectations.

- **Leadership.** Leaders establish the organizational direction and provide unity of purpose.

- **Engagement of people.** People are the core asset and purpose of the organization.

- **Process approach.** Results are achieved when activities, people, and resources are managed as an integrated process.

- **Improvement.** Continual improvement of all organizational elements is a permanent organizational objective.

- **Evidence based, decision making.** Effective and efficient decisions are based on data analysis and reliable information.

- **Relationship management.** An organization and its suppliers have interdependent processes that create stakeholder create.[2]

THE REGISTRATION PROCESS

ISO/TS 16949 is the U.S. auto industry version of the ISO 9001:2015. The Big Three automakers (Ford, GM and Chrysler) got together and added extra provisions to ISO 9001:2015. This created ISO/TS 16949, which first-tier suppliers are induced to meet. The eventual goal is to move this down the supply chain.

There is no right way to pursue ISO 9001:2015 registration. Registration is a doable task for many companies if a team and project management approach is followed. Like managing any complex project, such as ISO 9001:2015 registration, senior management must understand and approve the project; resources must be gathered and channeled to the appropriate locations and tasks; and supply stakeholders must see the benefits of the project.

The following are generalized steps for pursuing ISO 9001:2015 registration:

- **Step #1. Understand the ISO 9001:2015 registration environment.** ISO 9001:2015 registration is a global phenomenon. A company should understand what competitors are doing, what customer's want, and what regulatory authorities expect.

- **Step #2. Determine the benefits and challenges of ISO 9001:2015 registration.** ISO 9001:2015 registration isn't easy. A company pursuing ISO 9001:2015 registration or deploying quality systems should conduct a basic cost-benefit analysis of pursuing registration. ISO 9001:2015 can be pursued as a means to improve business operations or as a means to get 'their ticket punched'. In the latter case, the customer requires ISO registration to be on an approved bidders list. The supplier develops quality documents to appease the customer.

- **Step #3. Secure management commitment.** Senior management must be fully committed and authorize the necessary resources including people, monies, and equipment. Senior management must also actively participate in the registration by establishing project teams, maintaining organizational enthusiasm, providing direction, and reconciling differences. Middle management must be committed because they provide the members for the ISO 9001:2015 project team.

- **Step #4. Plan for ISO 9001:2015 registration.** ISO 9001:2015 registration should be thoroughly planned so resources are not wasted or the project team does not go down dead ends.

- **Step #5. Organize for registration.** Often, a multi-disciplinary project team tackles ISO 9001:2015 registration. The project team plans and develops quality system documentation. The team also verifies that processes and systems are in place and operating properly. The team ensures that registration is implemented on time, under budget, satisfies stakeholder requirements.

- **Step #6. Train, Train, Train.** New quality systems and other business processes are implemented. Audits are conducted. Corrective and prevention actions are implemented. Procedures and work instructions are written. All of this requires training.

- **Step #7. Conduct the preassessment.** The preassessment compares the 'what is' against the 'what shall be' as specified by the ISO 9001:2015. This is called ISO 9001:2015 document gap analysis or simply gap analysis.

- **Step #8. Flowchart processes and develop quality documentation.** Developing quality documentation and mapping processes are the most time consuming and expensive elements of ISO 9001:2015 registration. Three levels of ISO quality documentation are usually prepared, specifically quality manual policies, procedures, and work instructions.

- **Step #9. Select a registrar.** Trust, service, and responsiveness are probably the critical factors for selecting a registrar. The registrar is an independent third party that audits a company for compliance to ISO 9001:2015 criteria. This is largely a commodity service for which most registrars charge similar fees for similar services.

- **Step #10. Maintain registration.** Once a company secures registration, the company must actively maintain registration. ISO 9001:2015 registration is a long-term process of continuous auditing to ever-higher revised quality standards. The standards are revised every six to seven years incorporating higher quality and business process requirements. As well, the registrar conducts a surveillance audit of a company every six months or every year.[3]

SUMMARY

There has been an amazing proliferation of awards in the last ten years that are used as customer-supply certification standards. The notable American quality awards include: the Baldrige Performance Excellence Program and operational excellence awards.

ISO 9001:2015 is a global customer-supply certification standard. ISO quality documentation and quality system assessments are used to certify candidate suppliers. As suppliers move up the maturity curve, customers more often conduct process audits that relate directly to customer requirements and customer-supply integration.

CHAPTER 11:
SUPPLY DEVELOPMENT –
CONTINUOUS IMPROVEMENT

Customer and supplier differences will always arise. How these are corrected and prevented from recurring should be addressed early in the customer-supply relationship. I've seen that little differences in opinion and expectations can cause irreconcilable problems between the customer and supplier. If problems arise, then immediate follow up, joint problem solving and root-cause solution can cement the customer-supplier relationship.

In this chapter, we discuss how to analyze and improve the supply chain. Then, we offer a methodology for solving supply process problems.

SUPPLY CHAIN PROBLEM SOLVING

The first piece of intelligent tinkering is to save all the parts.
Paul Ehrlich

A supply chain consists of interrelated systems and processes such as information systems, logistics systems, financial systems, human resource information systems, planning processes, manufacturing systems, and quality systems. There are also a number of sub-supply systems including internal quality auditing, training, and customer service processes.

THE SUPPLY CHAIN SYSTEM

Systems theory can be used as the basis for supply chain problem solving. Systems problem solving grew out of general systems theory in the last 40 years. Systems theory attempted to define and solve problems by understanding the whole structure (supply chain) and then looking at each component (supplier). Each core internal process or system is understood as well as the interrelationships between the links of the supply chain.

UPSTREAM PRODUCT PROBLEM SOLVING

Let's look at enhancing supply chain value through one prism, quality or specifically product defect prevention. As a product is made or a service is delivered, value is added. Value is the labor, machinery, material, or facilities required to do work. Value is ensured at the source, not at the end of the process. For example, it is expensive to scrap a porous casting after it has gone through 10 or more manufacturing steps. Or, it is counter productive to manufacture a highly reliable product if the delivery system is inefficient.

However, quality as 'conformance to specifications' cannot be assured or controlled by inspecting quality into the product. Inspectors inspect, sort, rework, rehandle, and reinspect defective products. This is wasteful, because it consumes time, effort, expense, material, personnel, and facilities.

Likewise, customer satisfaction cannot be guaranteed by instructing a salesperson in courtesy after the sale. The salesperson or receptionist should have been instructed in policies and procedures before the assignment.

USING THE SYSTEMS APPROACH TO SOLVE SUPPLY CHAIN PROBLEMS

The supply chain must be broken down into its component parts. The supply chain process consists of many subprocesses and even miniprocesses consisting of many steps, each of which has an input and output. An internal supplier provides input to an internal customer who processes and outputs to an internal customer. Each process step adds value in the process chain. Each process step owner is responsible for the value of effort as well as ensuring that downstream customers are satisfied.

Supply chain problem solving can be incremental, continuous, and breakthrough. Regardless of the type, it follows a systematic and structured approach focusing on measurable, simple, and doable solutions.

It usually incorporates the following elements:

- Identify supply chain improvement project.

- Define problem risks and constraints.

- Organize to solve problem.

- Identify possible and probable causes.

- Select the best solution.

- Implement the solution.

- Audit improvements.

Identify Supply Chain Improvement Project
A supply chain improvement project is first identified. A project may involve customers or suppliers who have requirements, specifications, needs, or expectations, which are not being met. Or, a project may improve supply chain effectiveness, add product value, or minimize process variation.

Safety or health issues usually have the highest priority. Customer, market, chronic, major, and cost issues with the greatest potential for gain are then considered. The financial impact of each alternative project is estimated. These are determined by estimating the cost of achieving or not achieving a supply chain objective. Customer surveys, warranty claims, and customer complaints can also identify supply chain improvement projects.

Define Problem Risks and Constraints

Supply chain risks and constraints have to be identified. Risks or constraints are factors that may impede implementation of a solution. Constraints can be lack of financial resources, internal resistance, lack of special supply management skills or lack of measuring equipment.

Organize to Solve Problem

Supply management teams are the best approach to solve a problem. A multidisciplinary team has the requisite knowledge, skills, abilities, perspective, and resources to attack the supply wide problems. Supply management professionals usually facilitate or lead the team.

Identify Possible and Probable Causes

Specific supply chain or process owners are asked to participate in the solution. Those who are impacted by the problem have the best knowledge to identify probable causes. It's important to focus on root causes, not only problem symptoms. The root cause or causes may be people, material, methods or machinery or some combination of these.

Select the Best Solution

Once root causes are identified, solutions are proposed to eliminate the root cause. Brainstorming is one common technique of soliciting solutions from process owners. The 'best' solution is selected for implementation. Best may be the solution that is easiest to implement, leads to lower costs, removes supply chain constraints, enhances development time to market, etc.

Implement Solution

Implementation is often assigned to those responsible for the problem, the internal or supply process owners. Or, implementation may be assigned to the project team, who performs the work with the blessings of the process owners. Implementation can cross supply, departmental, or functional boundaries.

Audit Improvements

Supply chain improvement is measured to determine the impact of the intervention. Accrued benefits justify the next supply management improvement project. Improvement is then audited to ensure the root cause or causes are eliminated so the problem does not recur. Once root causes have been eliminated, a new level of performance, hopefully a breakthrough, has been attained.

Optimize Solution (Start Again)

Once this level has been attained, the supply chain problem solving process starts all over again on a new problem. Or, if not enough improvement has been achieved, the process repeats the above steps.

AUDIT PROCESS

The big things you can see with one eye closed. But keep both eyes wide open for the little things. Little things mark the great dividing line between success and failure.
Jacob Braude

Auditing, corrective action, and preventive action are probably the three most critical processes for improving supply performance. They 'close the loop' with all supply chain problem solving. They form the basis of monitoring, intervening, correcting, and improving most customer-supply processes.

ISO 9001:2015 AUDIT REQUIREMENTS

Auditing is a fundamental element of most capability maturity models, customer-supply partnering relationships and certification standards such as ISO 9001:2015. Suppliers are often required to designate a group of internal process and quality auditors.

ISO 9001:2015 states that audits "determine the extent to which the quality management system requirements are fulfilled."[1] The objective of internal auditing is to determine the effectiveness of the quality management system and identify opportunities for improvement.

CONTINUOUS SUPPLY CHAIN REVIEW

Customer-supply audits are one of the most effective monitoring and improvement techniques. Often, these assessments are called quality audits but also involve analysis of cost, technology, delivery, service and other factors. These audits are an official examination of supply chain processes, products, or people to verify process improvement, effectiveness, and compliance to policies, procedures, work instructions, and specifications. Audits can be conducted on a periodic or random basis and can be performed unannounced or upon request.

Auditing is also critical to all supply chains to ensure the right products are delivered to the right location on time, in the right sequence, properly protected. In other words, audits ensure key supply chain processes should be running smoothly, are controlled, are capable, and improving.

Once the audit is conducted, audit findings are documented in a report that is circulated to authorized clients. The audit report may recommend preventive action, corrective action or no action. Usually, if action is indicated, a corrective action request (CAR) or preventive action request (PAR) is written to initiate further action.

The following are advantages of conducting customer-supply audits:

- Provide independent and objective advice to management.

- Monitor customer-supply processes and products.

- Provide corrective action follow up.

- Identify areas of process improvement.

- Measure effectiveness of people, processes, product, and organizational improvement.[2]

AUDIT PROCESS STEPS

An audit, particularly a system audit, is a snapshot of a supplier at a given point in time. The supply chain is really a moving picture. The auditee (person or area being assessed) may present an over optimistic image that does not reflect supply chain realities. On the other hand, a minor problem can be blown out of proportion and may not accurately reflect the general conditions of the process.

Customer-supply, internal quality, certification, and risk audits follow a systematic process of:

- Preparation.

- Preliminary conference.

- Data acquisition.

- Data interpretation.

- Closing conference.

- Feedback and action.

- Root cause elimination.

Preparation

The auditee (the organization or supplier) is first notified of the impending audit. The auditee is advised when it will be conducted, who and how many people will be involved, and why it is being conducted.

The team obtains background information on the auditee. Background information is obtained from financial statements, previous audits, and trade journal articles. For specific information, the team evaluates the contract, quality manual, specifications, bills of material, drawings, layouts, flowcharts, reliability test reports, and customer service history.

Preliminary Conference

The preliminary conference at the auditee's facility establishes audit ground rules. Any auditee fears are dispelled in this conference.

Data Acquisition
The audit team or auditor collects program, process, people, and product information. The team interviews management and employees. The team reviews quality, policies, quality procedures, product plans, cost, technical capabilities, and specifications.

Data Interpretation
The team interprets evidence and data collected during the audit. This is time consuming and labor intensive. The team should understand the client's industry, internal processes, and products.   With this knowledge, the team attempts to identify unusual variations, risks, constraints, or waste and may recommend corrective or preventive actions.

Closing Conference
The closing conference reviews preliminary impressions, problems, conclusions, and recommendations. If there are substantive areas of disagreement, these may be appealed to the customer's corporate management.

Feedback and Action
Finally, the auditee is formally notified in writing of audit results. If deficiencies are found, the auditee (the supplier) is asked to correct them prior to approval of shipment of products. If the auditee does not agree with the recommendations and conclusions, then customer and auditee (supplier) management may resolve the differences.

If the supplier is being evaluated for the first time, the audit team may approve the supplier, reject the supplier, or recommend further evaluation. If the supplier has been supplying products for some time, the audit is used as a monitoring tool to encourage continuous improvement.

Root Cause Elimination
Root cause analysis investigates the cause and the chain of events that resulted in the problem. Each critical process step is assessed, possible causes are identified and examined until a root cause is determined.

Once this process becomes institutionalized, supply chain problem solving becomes a normal course of business. The challenge is a problem may have multiple causes, which make it difficult to determine the prime cause in a supply chain consisting of many sub-tier suppliers.

The supply or quality manager in an audit should not take the role of process owner. The process owner may be a supplier who is still responsible for the process or project solution. The supply manager can advise but the owner must decide on and implement the solution.

AUDIT DATA ANALYSIS

Audit analysis can reveal risks, variances, nonconformances, and opportunities for improvement, as indicated by the following:

- **Risk analysis.** Areas of high risk and internal controls to minimize or eliminate the risks are identified.

- **Cost analysis.** Process, product, customer, and operational cost variance analysis may indicate opportunities for improvement.

- **Type and number of deficiencies (nonconformances).** Deficiencies can be a customer complaint, cost variance, ISO 9001:2015 noncompliance, or product field failure. This data may indicate if the problem is isolated or if it is an early warning of a widespread problem.

- **Location of deficiency.** The location of the deficiency reveals if a problem is isolated to a specific location, gage, or application or is a chronic widespread problem. This data when collated or analyzed can provide more clues for isolating the problem and determining the root-cause.

- **Corrective action analysis.** Corrective action analysis determines if actions to eliminate the cause of the deficiency were successful.

- **Preventive action analysis.** Preventive action analysis is a proactive analysis of data such as supplier records, quality results, service reports and customer complaints to detect, analyze, and eliminate causes of probable deficiencies.

TREND ANALYSIS

Trend analysis is a simple monitoring and analysis tool to determine if supply chain processes are stable, capable, and even improving. Trend analysis can detect a pending or potential problem. Typical examples of problem trends include high rework, customer service reports, high product waivers, continued inspection and high waste levels. The figure on the next page, 'Continuous Improvement Examples,' illustrates several examples of improving trends.

Trend and data analysis reveal audit, corrective action, and preventive action effectiveness. If supply deficiencies or problems continue, this indicates the symptom was fixed but the root cause of the problem was not discovered and eliminated. When a deficiency or nonconformance is discovered, the problem and data are entered into a database for future examination. Did the problem recur? How often and in what area did it recur? Could the recurrence be due to multiple factors?

CORRECTION AND PREVENTION

Problem solving and constructive innovation are what business is all about.
Randall Meyer

If the audit finds no deficiencies, then the audit findings report this. If the audit finds deficiencies then corrective and/or prevention actions are recommended.

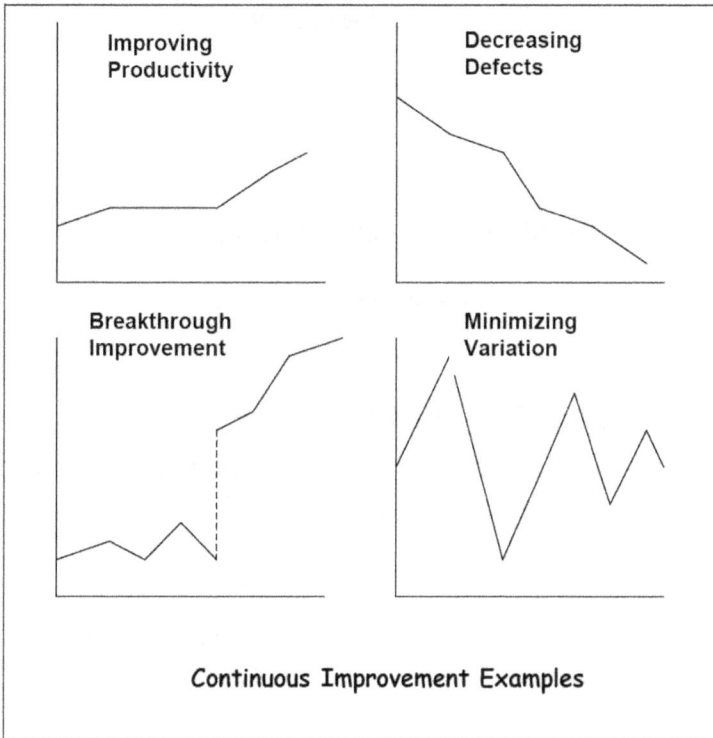

Continuous Improvement Examples

Corrective and preventive actions are essential elements of all supply chain problem solving. Corrective and preventive actions ensure symptoms as well as their root causes are eliminated so supply problems don't recur.

WHAT IS CORRECTIVE ACTION?

According to the ISO 9001:2015, corrective action is "the need for action to eliminate the cause(s) of the nonconformity, in order that it does not recur or occur elsewhere, by:

- Reviewing and analyzing the nonconformity.

- Determining the causes of the nonconformity.

- Determining if similar nonconformities exist, or could potentially occur.[3]

Corrective action may involve:

- Redesigning or modifying the product.

- Redesigning or modifying fixtures and dies.

- Training suppliers.

- Updating specifications or changing tolerances.

- Increasing incoming material inspection.

MANAGING SUPPLY DIFFERENCES

Successful collaborative negotiation lies in finding out what the other side really wants and showing them a way to get it, while you get what you want. **Herb Cohen**

Even in the best of supply chain relationships, problems can arise. These challenges are opportunities to build long term trust.

PROBLEMS CAN ARISE ANYWHERE, ANY TIME

We often think the source of a problem is the supplier. But, either the customer or supplier can be the source. The customer can modify a drawing so the supplier can no longer make the part. The customer may want a sudden increase of products shipped to the plant, but the supplier is already running three shifts at capacity. The customer may tighten specifications and tolerances so the supplier can't make the product. This occurs when the customer wants improved quality and reliability too quickly and the supplier does not have the internal capability to make products to specification.

The supplier can also have problems. A supplier can be on strike or can have fire, capacity, financial, or even supply problems of its own. Any of these can disrupt or stop the supply chain.

CONTEXT: SCM Process Improvement

- Measure, compare, and report on supply chain performance over time.
- Monitor events in real time, including inventory levels and shipments.
- Notify proactively a decision maker that intervention, correction, and prevention have to be taken.
- Simulate or create what-if scenarios based on those events.
- Continuously monitor and control the supply chain.[4]

WHEN IT HITS THE FAN!

There are a number of early indicators of supply chain trouble. Costs are high. Chain is unstable. Processes are not capable. Inventories creep up. Stakeholders are unhappy. Customer satisfaction is low. Field failures are high. It is critical to quickly understand the supply chain problem and pinpoint its root cause. Then a supply management team can be assembled and follow the 'Supply Chain Problem Solving' methodology discussed earlier in the chapter.

It's assumed that partners are voluntarily participating and have agreed to jointly solve/fix problems. However, a sub supplier in a sub chain may not be as disposed as a first-tier supplier to readily root cause fix problems. We call this a problem supplier.

A problem supplier is one who is unresponsive. A problem supplier is thus monitored or audited more closely than other suppliers. Close monitoring may involve more frequent plant visits to intensified process monitoring. Close monitoring usually ends when the supplier has shipped acceptable products over a period of time. If nonconforming products continue to be shipped, the supplier is trained, induced or finally removed from the approved supplier's list.

WORKING WITH SUPPLIERS

So, what can be done with problem or recalcitrant suppliers? Dispute resolution systems and procedures have to be established so differences can be readily settled. Companies can pursue the following options:

- Work with existing suppliers.

- Manufacture component in house.

- Find new suppliers.

Work with Existing Suppliers

If more products, tighter tolerances, lower prices, and faster delivery are needed, the preferred option is to work with existing suppliers. Existing suppliers already know customer needs and wants. If the customer anticipates the need for more products and the supplier is running at full capacity or the supplier cannot manufacture products to specifications then the customer may provide the supplier with financial and technical incentives.

Manufacture Component In-House

A less preferred option may be to develop the internal capability or competency to manufacture the component. This is done if the supplier cannot consistently make conforming products because of material, technology, cost, or personnel problems. Critical or state-of-the-art products may require additional investment in property, plant, equipment, and extensive personnel training.

Find a New Supplier

The third option is to find a new supplier. The process of evaluating and selecting a new supplier was covered earlier. The process is long and tedious, so it is less preferred than inducing, training, and negotiating with existing suppliers.

Finding a new supplier is difficult. Think of all the things that must be done to establish the level of trust that existing suppliers have. That's why companies prefer to help their existing suppliers improve rather than locate, qualify, and switch to alternates.

Customer-supply collaboration implies both parties will attack problems through joint problem-solving teams, will identify root causes, will experiment to identify sources of variation, and will implement supply chain improvements. Benefits are then shared equally between customer and supplier.[5]

As we discussed, customers will change suppliers when the pain of changing suppliers is less than working with a supplier. What would induce a company to look for a new supplier? The customer may want to:

- Improve supplier delivery, cost and quality.

- Reduce inspection or rework.

- Lower prices and overall costs.

- Improve supply metrics.

RESOLVING CUSTOMER-SUPPLY CONFLICTS

Supply chain conflicts always arise and can be resolved basically in three ways:

- Litigate.

- Accept.

- Negotiate.

Litigate

The least-preferred option is to rely on lawyers and the courts to settle differences. Litigation is expensive and requires time to adjudicate and, unfortunately, the outcome is usually ill-will between parties.

Accept

Another option is to accept the problem. Not resolving disputes or problems in the short-term results in larger, long term problems. A TV commercial sums up the situation by warning 'pay me now or pay me later.' When problems festered for years, the only way to resolve a dispute may be through litigation and the cost of litigation can threaten a firm's survival.

Negotiate

The preferred option is to negotiate or arbitrate differences. Differences then can be resolved quickly and inexpensively. A win-win partnership can slowly evolve where the customer gets quality products delivered just in time and the supplier gets a long-term contract.[6]

SUMMARY

The basic theme of this chapter is that all supply chain processes should be improved over time. Supply managers must know the basic process auditing tools, speak the language of supply development, and know internal/supplier process capabilities. As well, supply managers must be sensitive to different organizational cultures. Supply managers also assume different roles during supply development and may serve as auditors and even internal consultants.

CHAPTER 12:
SUPPLY DEVELOPMENT –
MEASUREMENT

'Measurement is critical to all SCM decision making. Measurements provide a foundation for the customer-supply relationship and development.

Many North American companies have established partnering arrangements with their suppliers to improve product and service performance. Traditional customer-supply relationships were based on anecdotal evidence to draw conclusions about supplier quality, cost, delivery, and technology. The trend now is to rely on real time objective, verifiable, and measurable information upon which to base supply chain partnering and purchase decisions.

BUSINESS METRICS

Times change and we change.
Latin Proverb

Supply chain business metrics and drivers start at the top of the organization. Corporate goals are first established and then are communicated to employees and key supply-partners. Goals and objectives are then established throughout the supply chain. Supplier daily, weekly, monthly, quarterly, and yearly improvements are measured towards meeting these objectives. At the lowest, transactional or activity level on the assembly line or with the receptionist, progress may be measured on a monthly, weekly, or daily basis.

SUPPLY MEASURES ARE BUSINESS MEASURES

Increasing supplier performance is now considered part of the competitiveness equation. Five years ago, supply measures weren't on the radar screen. Now, senior management wants supply chain metrics. Supply managers must understand what drives senior management. This is the first step to 'management speak.'

The Chief Purchasing Officer (CPO) usually leads the strategic sourcing discussion with senior management. However, supply managers must be able to demonstrate and explain how the supply chain impacts the bottom line.

Key performance indicators often include:

- **Financial measures.** Financial measures are the most critical supply performance measures. Performance indicators such as income, return on equity, and growth in book value indicate the company can fulfill its obligations, invest for growth, and reduce debt through strong assets and strong cash flow. Financial performance is usually compared against companies in the same industry sector or Standard and Poor's 500. Supply managers must demonstrate how a streamlined supply chain improves business financial measures.

- **Shareholder value.** Supply chain contribution to shareholder value is another important indicator to senior management of a company's competitive health. Shareholders expect a return consistent with their expectations and risk. If they don't receive the supply chain returns they expect, they will move their assets to another company. The Darwinian message is crystal clear to management, to continually appreciate stock value, dramatically cut supply chain costs, develop products quickly, and meet ever rising customer expectations.

- **Percentage of total sales.** Total or increasing sales indicate that company is growing. The supply chain is expected to contribute to this in demonstrable ways. Sales outside the U.S. are an important factor for many businesses because many domestic markets are mature and exhibit slow growth.

- **Customer satisfaction.** Customer satisfaction delivered through the supply chain is another important measure of a company's performance. Studies indicate that customer satisfaction and profitability tend to be positively correlated.

- **Market entry.** New market expansion indicates the company is searching for new growth opportunities. With reduced lifecycles, stagnant markets, and competitive pressures, senior management expects supply chain initiatives to lower costs and facilitate growth in new markets.

- **Market diversification.** Diversification of supply chain risks minimizes market, competitive, and customer risks.

- **New product development.** High quality, new products, and services are the foundation for a company's continued profitability. Time to market is an essential strategic metric to supply management. Without new products, a company's competitiveness withers.

- **Core competencies.** A company's core supply chain strengths allow it to lever its ability to develop new products, enter new markets, and develop new applications.

- **Reputation.** Perceptions of quality, excellence, profitability, and efficiency are sometimes just as important as their reality. So, companies enhance their brand reputation through consistent advertising, promotions, and public services up and down the supply chain.

SUPPLY CHAIN METRICS

Success, as I see it, is a result, not a goal.
Gustave Flaubert, Writer

More often, supply management objectives and measures are placed in the performance appraisals of people outside the function.

INTERNAL SUPPLY MANAGEMENT METRICS

In the last several years, supply chain objectives were only incorporated in the compensation and performance plans of senior supply management. Since supply management is an all-inclusive function, we're seeing materials, quality, planning, engineering, and manufacturing managers have supply performance measures. One driver of this trend is to bring organizational silos and suppliers closer together.

KEY SUPPLY PERFORMANCE INDICATORS

Measurement is essential to supply development. Without complete and accurate data, decisions cannot be made of a supplier's performance. Supply metrics also must be tailored to the maturity of the supply chain and to the capability of the specific supplier.

Many supply chain measures deal with manufacturing process control. What does this mean? Supply chain teams and process personnel attempt to proceduralize and stabilize operations that are capable of satisfying customer requirements. If there is an unusual occurrence, the supply process is stopped and the source of the problem is discovered and eliminated. Control depends on process owners using their best judgment to make the right decisions to solve the problem.

EXAMPLES OF SUPPLY PERFORMANCE METRICS

Common measures used to track and monitor suppliers include:

Supply Quality Metrics

Examples of supply quality measures include:

- Process capabilities.

- Product quality performance.

- Production line performance.

- Reliability performance.

- Customer returns.

- Corrective action responsiveness.

- Parts per million quality levels (six sigma).

- Rejects of incoming material.

- Rework in dollars or hours.

- Production stoppages.

- End customer complaints.

- Recurring nonconformances.

- Amount of material accepted on-waivers.

- Number of late shipments.

- Tighter specifications.

- Technical competency.

Supply Service Metrics

Examples of supply service measures include:

- Proven service leadership.

- Willingness to partner.

- Pricing and cost reduction commitments within customer expectations.

- Favorable payment terms.

CONTEXT: Supply Measurement Benefits

- Conveys customer requirements and inducements throughout the supply chain.
- Establishes agreed upon means to develop the customer-supply relationship.
- Establishes supply baselines for quality, cost, and delivery.
- Helps to develop supplier performance benchmarks and opportunities.
- Creates improvement opportunities.
- Assists both customer and supplier to improve performance through a gap analysis.
- Identifies customer-supply quality, cost, and schedule trends.
- Identifies the best suppliers to work with and to move up the capability curve.
- Identifies where to commit limited resources.
- Is a means to evaluate the overall supply chain efficiency, economics, and effectiveness.

- Availability of products.

- Flexibility in schedules.

- JIT processes in manufacturing and material control.

- Local inventory points.

- Ease of doing business and communications.

Supply Support Metrics
Examples of supply support measures include:

- Help desk capabilities.

- Design methodology.

- Product engineering/development support.

- Early supply involvement.

- Concurrent engineering commitment.

- Product time-to-market development schedules.

- Supply quality assurance support.

- Supply open and honest communications.

- Service development responsiveness.

Supply Financial Metrics
- Economic value added.

- Total cost reductions.

- Scrap costs generated in use.

- Warranty costs due to product failure.

- Cost of doing business in the development process.

- Sourcing life cycle cost reduction.

- Maintenance costs reduction.

- Equipment warranty cost reduction.

- Disposal cost.

- Sourcing transaction cost reduction.

- Inventory costs reduction.

- Equipment uptime and share cost reduction.

BALANCED SCORECARD

Supply management scorecards are used to evaluate supplier performance. The idea behind balanced scorecards is that customer and supplier interactions are graded based on a mutually established measurement method and based on the criticality of the product. For example, high value goods and services would be evaluated by different criteria and weighted differently than commodity items.

Then throughout the contract or product lifecycle, transaction events, processes, products, or shipments are evaluated on process and value based criteria. Does this mean the customer develops a new set of standards or criteria for each supplier? No. The customer and supplier negotiate the criteria based on the product risks.[1]

How effective is this method? Traditionally, the customer measured supplier performance based on a one-way scorecard. The customer imposed these on a critical few or all suppliers. This sometimes worked great or it was simply window dressing for one-way customer demands upon the supplier. It's hoped that the new balanced scorecard, like 360-degree human resource performance evaluations, would be more fair and balanced.

BOEING SUPPLY CERTIFICATION

Most *Fortune 1000* companies have a supply certification or rating program. They are based on a graded report card or on a weighted average numerical rating system. Boeing for example has a 'preferred supplier certification' process where suppliers are evaluated and rated against specific standards in statistical process control, business processes and performance. The best suppliers are recognized publicly. In 1999, only 116 of Boeing's 3100 suppliers were recognized and just 13 were given 'supplier of the year' recognition.[2]

AGGRESSIVE SUPPLY CHAIN METRICS

If you don't measure it, you can't manage it and it won't happen.
Anonymous

More customers are developing aggressive supply cost, delivery, and quality metrics. Usually, these stretch metrics are called lean or six sigma metrics. For example, Chrysler is expecting 15% cost reduction from suppliers. GE expects six sigma (parts per million) quality levels from service and product suppliers. And, the list goes on.

INCREMENTAL OR AGGRESSIVE BENCHMARKS

There is a big debate whether supply chain performance improvement should be incremental or aggressive. Continuous process improvement is based on a series of singles winning the supply chain ball game. Improvements are regular and focused on things that matter to the customer. Some say, that incremental improvement is necessary but not sufficient in a highly competitive marketplace that rewards first movers, first developers, and first to critical mass.

The benefit with incremental improvement is that there are fewer surprises for the customer and the supplier. The counter argument is that incremental improvement can breed relaxation and mediocrity over the long term. Stretch benchmarks can be used as a means to encourage flexibility, innovation, and performance improvement. The customer can then rate multiple suppliers to reduce the supply base.

PERFORMANCE RULES: RISE OF ACCOUNTABLE METRICS

Jack Welch, the former CEO of GE, was the nameplate leader for much of the last decade. What made him so effective? He always focused on performance. One person who worked for Welch said every limo or elevator ride would be an opportunity for a performance review. "A general manager's quarterly and year-to-date profit and loss variance analysis takes minutes. And the variance is measured not against the budget but against what the manager had promised."[3]

"The chairman and chief executive of Union Carbide Corp., in an unusual move, bet on his company's performance, agreed to forfeit a year's salary if the chemicals company doesn't meet its earnings target according to a *The Wall Street Journal* article.[4] Would you put your salary at risk?

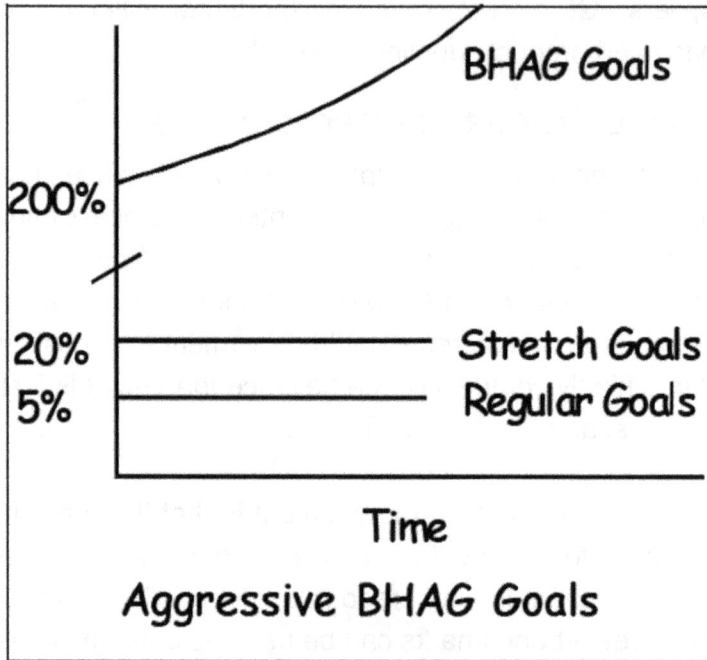

Aggressive BHAG Goals

What does this mean to supply managers? Union Carbide's Chairman's decision to put his salary at risk isn't lost on shareholders, competition, and suppliers. Usually, entrepreneurs put their salary and future at risk. Now, we're hearing more about 'shared risk - shared reward' in more work and supply chain environments. More supply managers and employees are putting real pay on the line and are betting stock options and bonuses on their success - in other words, more supply managers are being asked to 'walk their talk.' More organizations, more than 51%, tie non-management and non-sales personnel compensation to individual or group performance.[5]

This is part of a larger trend. Entitlement is dead - accountability is alive and well. Everyone in the supply chain is responsible for their activity, process, function, team, plant, and company performance. Performance management is a direct outcome of self-management and self managed supply teams. Senior management is looking to supply chain process owners to operationalize the critical elements of the strategic vision, mission, plans, objectives, etc. Each supply manager is now expected to know how his or her contributions fit into the organization's overall goals and how they meet customer requirements.

CONTEXT: Harley-Davidson (H-D) Supply Metrics

- Improve service.
- Onsite representation (24-hour, seven-day accessibility).
- One-stop shopping of MRO items for customers.
- Increase on-the-floor technical support.
- Integrate effectively into the H-D organization.
- Serve as a support function for high performance work teams.
- Provide information and education to allow users to make better decisions.
- Reduce supply chain and life cycle costs.
- Formalize process to identify and implement savings utilizing cross-functional involvement.
- Standardize products, services and processes used across the H-D enterprise.
- Identify and achieve improvements based on operational integrity upgrades.
- Achieve diversity goals.

BIG HAIRY AUDACIOUS SCM GOALS (BHAG)

BHAG - what a strange acronym? BHAG (pronounced bee-hag) stands for Big Hairy Audacious Goals. Collins and Porras in **Built to Last** call super stretch performance goals BHAGs. Examples of BHAGs include IBM's decision to build the 360 computer and Facebook's decision to be the world's biggest social network. Both were outstandingly successful and set both firms apart in their respective industries.

BHAGs also identify superior suppliers. What characterizes a BHAG? It's a stretch goal, an opportunity, bigger than life that inspires people to actualize a vision. A BHAG should be doable and definitely stretch the current paradigm of do ability.[6] Today's supply managers are expected to destroy the current purchasing paradigms, burst today's envelope, and stretch way beyond the norm.

DAIMLER CHRYSLER SUPPLIER METRICS

Daimler Chrysler management wanted immediate action to stem the flood of red ink. Since so much of the manufacturing dollar resided in the supply base, Daimler Chrysler followed a 2-step process. In the first year, suppliers were directed to reduce by 5% the prices for materials and services. In the following years, Daimler Chrysler wanted to reduce costs another 10%.

How did they do this? The additional 10% in cost savings was expected to come from customer-supply partnering arrangements. Customer-supply teams, representing 75% of Daimler-Chrysler's material purchases, would work together to identify cost improvement areas.[7]

SUMMARY

Supply chain management is all about measuring internal as well as supply performance. One-sided SCM measures can cause problems. Trust is gained through mutual wins. Unfortunately, the reengineering and downsizing craze that hit the supply chain several years ago and continues today fractured much good will between customers and suppliers. Many companies reduced their supply bases by 50% or more. As well, many suppliers became cynical as they discovered that many companies imposed requirements that customers didn't follow themselves. Suppliers said that the customer-supply relationship was one sided. In other words, 'do as I say, don't do as I do' bred cynicism.

CHAPTER 13: INTRODUCTION TO SUPPLY RISK MANAGEMENT

Risk management is a systematic process of managing unwanted events or unwanted change. Sound familiar? Supply chain management is fundamentally risk management.

WHAT IS RISK?

All business proceeds on beliefs or judgments of probabilities, and not on certainties.
Unknown

Risks are inherent in any customer-supply contract, project, or process. Smart risk management or smart supply chain management is the ability of not being blindsided by unexpected events. Smart supply managers want to avoid supply crises, firefighting, or reactive management. It's smart decision making to have stable supply processes, focus resources on the areas of highest risk, and manage by exception.

BUSINESS TODAY IS ALL ABOUT MANAGING RISK

The American Management Association said this about risk:

> "For virtually every business in the United States, the implications of economic change are enormous. The rapidly changing and more uncertain environment not only has made corporate decision-making and planning more difficult, but also has significantly increased business risks. Operating successfully in this

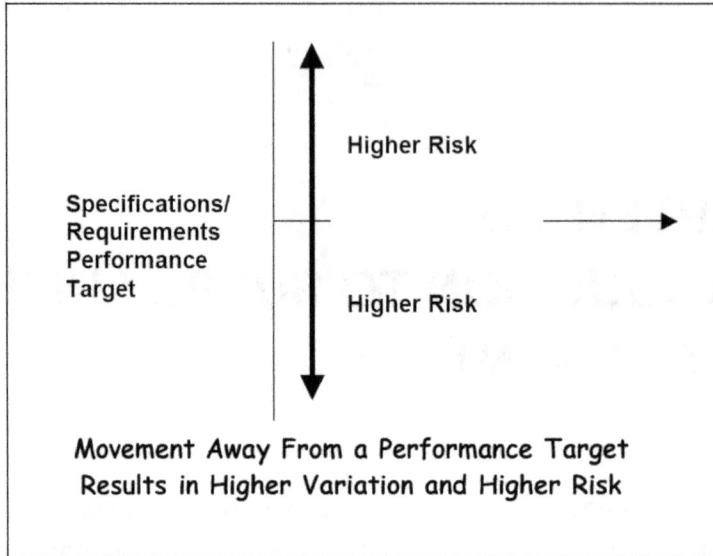

Movement Away From a Performance Target
Results in Higher Variation and Higher Risk

new environment will require a very different approach to business management. It involves more, rather than less, attention to external factors, as well as new priorities and strategies and a sharply increased focus on risk management."[1]

WHAT IS RISK?

Understanding and minimizing risk has become a best practice for all companies. There are many definitions of risk. Risk may be the occurrence of an unwanted event. It may be a deviation or variance from a target or norm, which may be a technical specification, contract, or engineering drawing (See above figure).

The Institute of Internal Auditors defines risk as:

> "… the probability that an event or action may adversely affect the organization or activity under review."[2]

The following are common elements of most risk definitions:

- Ability to meet contract, process, and product requirements.

- Possibility of harm or loss if requirements are not achieved.

```
          ┃
          ┃
          ┃
   High    ┃  Electronic      │  Electronic
   Value   ┃  Chips in        │  Chips in
          ┃  Household       │  Regulated
          ┃  Appliances      │  Products
          ┃                  │
          ┃ ─ ─ ─ ─ ─ ─ ─ ─ ─│─ ─ ─ ─ ─ ─ ─ ─
          ┃                  │
   Low     ┃                  │
   Value   ┃  MRO             │  Fasteners in
          ┃  Products        │  Regulated
          ┃                  │  Products
          ┃                  │
          ┃                  │
          ┗━━━━━━━━━━━━━━━━━━━━━━━━━━━━━━━━━━▶

              Low Risk            High Risk

            Value/Risk Purchasing
```

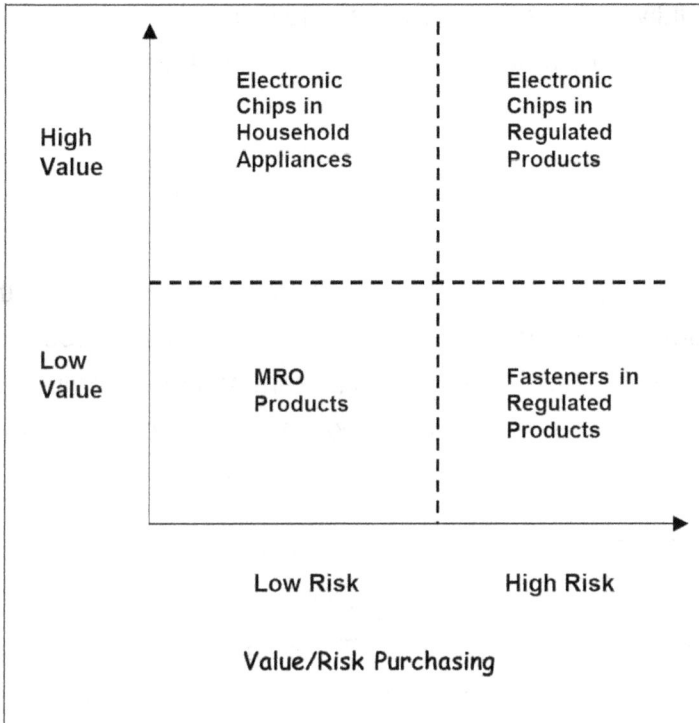

- Probability of an undesirable event with consequences.

- Variation away from a specification or requirement is monitored and controlled.

- Risk management is preferred over containment.

SUPPLY CHAIN RISKS

Many supply chain decisions come down to determining the acceptable level of risk from a make/buy decision to finding a new supplier to deciding on a 'sole source' supplier. Let's look at the risk of choosing a 'sole source' supplier.

The risk of having a 'sole source' supplier must be balanced against having multiple suppliers. While it is easier to manage one supplier, this decision entails higher risks. There is a possibility of an act of god, such as tornado or a strike. What are the consequences of these events occurring? On the other hand, multiple suppliers must be managed more carefully than a single supplier. Multiple or offshore suppliers also require more effort, resources, and time to manage.

Supply chain risk management can be as simple as evaluating value and risk or benefits and costs using a simple grid shown in the 'Value/Risk Purchasing' figure on the previous page. The supply manager would place the sourced products in the grid. Those at the upper right quadrant would be managed more carefully than those in lower left quadrant. While this is a simple risk management example, this logic would be used in more sophisticated analysis involving many product and service suppliers.

SUPPLY CHAIN RISK MANAGEMENT PROCESS

Normally, one doesn't think of supply management in the same breath as risk management. Well, it is. Throughout the contract or product lifecycle, the supply manager must:

- Identify risks.

- Analyze risk impacts.

- Control risks.

- Manage risks.

We discuss each in the following sections.

IDENTIFY SUPPLY CHAIN RISKS

There's no such thing as 'zero risk'.
William Driver

The supply manager throughout the product development lifecycle should understand the supply chain's and specific supplier's risk profile. What do I mean? The supply team would first identify critical customer needs and operationalize these requirements through the supply chain.

The supply team would then identify supply constraints, variances, and weaknesses to satisfying these requirements. The supply chain manager can then do the same with each supplier, prioritizing risks of an unwanted event occurring. The team would then develop a plan to monitor, prevent, and if necessary mitigate the consequences of the supply chain risk event.

WHAT IMPACTS RISK?

To a large extent, risk is based on perceptions of what may occur and the impact of that occurrence. The supply manager or person has the knowledge to understand supply chain processes and assess risks. A number of factors can affect the supply manager's perception of risk, including:

- Supply chain processes.

- Supply chain controls.

- Supply chain maturity and capability.

- History of deliveries.

- Process management, assurance, and controls.

- Policies, procedures, and instructions.

- Product nonconformances.

- Amount of information available.

RISK IDENTIFICATION PROCESS

At a simple level, supply chain risk can be understood by identifying possible sources of unwanted variation from defined targets. In other words, the supply chain is a system composed of a number of processes and subprocesses. Possible risks are identified and controls should be in place to mitigate the risks.

The following are steps for identifying supply chain risks:

> **CONTEXT: Supply Chain Risk Management**
>
> - Deciding on a supply chain business model.
> - Determining whether to insource or to outsource.
> - Determining the optimal product mix to outsource.
> - Determining supply process capability and maturity levels.
> - Ensuring consistent delivery of critical parts.
> - Ensuring supply control points work.
> - Deciding on a 'push' or 'pull' demand system
> - Determining appropriate SCM software.
> - Determining appropriate preventive and corrective actions.
> - Designing win/win contracts with suppliers.
> - Anticipating and controlling undesirable logistics events.
> - Avoiding and mitigating product recalls.

- Flowchart the overall supply chain and sub processes.

- Define critical supply chain system, process, and product activities.

- Identify probable and possible sources of unwanted variation.

- Identify which sources of variation represent higher levels of risk.

- Develop system, process or product control points to prevent nonconformances.

- Monitor the controls.

- Intervene, correct, and prevent if unusual trends, nonconformances, or unwanted variation occurs.

TWO ELEMENTS OF RISK QUANTIFICATION

There are two fundamental elements of risk: 1. the probability of an unwanted occurrence and 2. the impact of the occurrence or exposure.

For example, there may be a 5% probability or chance of a relatively minor occurrence. This occurrence has little impact on the process, project, or product. On the other hand, a 1% probability of a major occurrence such as the inability to meet a delivery window would close down a plant. This is clearly unacceptable. Or, a 1% chance of occurrence of a life-threatening event is much too high and should be mitigated.

WHO SHOULD IDENTIFY RISK?

Most supply processes have only four or five critical risk variables. These can be analyzed, controlled and made capable relatively simply. On the other hand, some high value-added process steps may involve dozens of risk variables. These can be analyzed and understood through sophisticated statistical techniques such as Design of Experiments.

The process owner is responsible for identifying and managing his or her key process variables. This isn't the job of the quality or supply management organization. For example, a process may be transportation, machine or operator dependent. In an operator dependent process, the supply manager would spend his or her time evaluating how process owners assure stability, control capability, and pursue improvement. The supply manager again doesn't own the process. The supply manager wants verification the process is controlled and capable of meeting customer requirements. The supply manager may also want independent certification such as ISO 9001:2015 registration to confirm the validity of what the supplier says.

Hopefully, the process owners have identified quantified their process risks. More probably, the supply manager will introduce these concepts and work with the process owners to implement risk analysis into their processes.

```
┌─────────────────────────────────────────────────────────┐
│  CONTEXT: Risk Identification Tips                        │
│                                                           │
│   •  Identify supply events that may occur.               │
│   •  Estimate the likelihood of the event.                │
│   •  Identify consequences of the event.                  │
│   •  Know what's critical in the project or process.      │
│   •  Know what opportunities to pursue.                   │
│   •  Know what threats to address.                        │
└─────────────────────────────────────────────────────────┘
```

ANALYZE SUPPLY CHAIN RISK IMPACTS

Change can come with breathtaking speed, leaving a company on the defensive and in financial trouble when it's forced to catch up.
Gary Goldstick, Businessperson

Once the risks, consequences, and probability of the risks occurring are understood, then the supply management team can develop an overall supply chain and individual supplier risk profiles. The profiles prioritize risk areas and variables from highest to lowest. Using the Pareto Principle, the supply manager knows that 20 percent of the supply chain variables create 80 percent of the unwanted variation and 80 percent of the risk. The supply manager would then focus his or her attention on the areas of highest risk and ensure there are sufficient controls to minimize risks.

The Institute of Internal Auditors (the IIA) said the following about risk analysis:

> "Risk assessment is a systematic process for assessing and integrating professional judgments about probably adverse conditions and/or events. The risk assessment process should provide a means of organizing and integrating professional judgments for development of the organization's work schedule."[3]

There are many process and project risk related impacts. Most deal with some variance from a defined target. For example, supply chain risks include variances in:

- Schedule.

- Cost.

- Quality.

- Scope.

- Technology.

- Contracts.

And there are subset risks to each of these. For example, schedule related risks may involve the following unacceptable variation:

- Early shipments.

- Late shipments.

- Wrong location of shipment.

- Incorrect or inappropriate carrier.

- Incorrect product sequencing.

VARIANCE ANALYSIS

The SCM goal is to develop lean, continuous, and smooth supply processes. As a general rule, whenever there is a critical change in a process variable, the reason and cause of the change should be understood and analyzed. Why? The change in a critical supply process variable can have unwanted consequences and can cause risks to other elements of the integrated supply chain.

CONTEXT: When Should the Supply Manager Quantify Risk?

- High probability of risk occurrence or exposure.
- High impact of the risk occurrence or exposure.
- Life, safety, or environmentally threatening event.
- Customer or market condition changes.
- Major changes in the input variables in a supply chain process, including changes in personnel, management, environment, materials, suppliers, etc.
- Process instability or lack of capability of meeting requirements.
- Significant misunderstanding, variables, or other factors that change significant processes.

So whenever there is a change in a key process variable, the process owners should revisit the process to ensure it continues to be stable and capable. The new process variable can destabilize the process by creating unexpected variation, which can produce unexpected circumstances and higher risk, such as stop production and create the 'bullwhip' effect discussed in earlier chapters. Some unexpected variables can be:

- New carrier.

- New source of materials.

- New or untrained workers.

- New distributor.

The supply manager may well have developed supply system, process and product metrics. Variance from these measurements also indicates risk. Variances in system metrics such as ISO 9001:2015 or ISO/TS 16949 certification would indicate that policy and procedural controls are not in place and not being followed. Variances in process metrics such as capability indices would indicate that processes may not be in control or not capable of meeting customer requirements. Variances in product maintainability and reliability metrics would indicate the product may not be within dimensional specifications or performance requirements.

CONTROL SUPPLY CHAIN RISKS

All business proceeds on beliefs or judgments of probabilities, and not on certainties.
Charles Eliot, President Harvard University

Once risks are identified, risks must be controlled.

WHAT IS SCM CONTROL?

Supply management wants to control supply risks so the organization can be reasonably assured that business objectives can be met. Supply controls attempt to assure:

- Effectiveness and efficiency of supply chain processes.

- Reliability of financial reporting.

- Compliance with applicable laws and regulations.[4]

There are some important implications about controlling supply chain risks:

- Control is a process. It is a means to an end, not an end in itself.

- Control is conducted by people. It's not merely policy manuals and forms, but people at every level of an organization and the supply chain being responsible for their work.

- Control can be expected to provide only *reasonable assurance,* not absolute assurance to senior management.

- Control is geared to the achievement of objectives in internal and overlapping SCM processes.[5]

MANAGE SUPPLY CHAIN RISKS

Practice what you preach.
Plautus, Roman Playwright

Once the supply process is stable, meeting its objectives, and improving around performance targets, the supply manager can manage by exception instead of 'fighting fires.'

RISK MANAGEMENT PROCESS

As supply problems arise, the supply manager would follow a systematic process to correct and prevent their recurrence. The supply manager would follow these steps:

- Identify risks.

- Prioritize risks.

- Assess liabilities in case of a life, environmental, or safety incident.

- Develop emergency response for each specific risk area.

- Develop backup plans if there is a process or project shutdown.

- Develop contingent reserves for monies, resources, suppliers, people, etc.

- Test the contingencies.

- Document recommendations.

- Develop process or product metrics.

- Develop workarounds.

- Monitor system the supply process or project intervention.

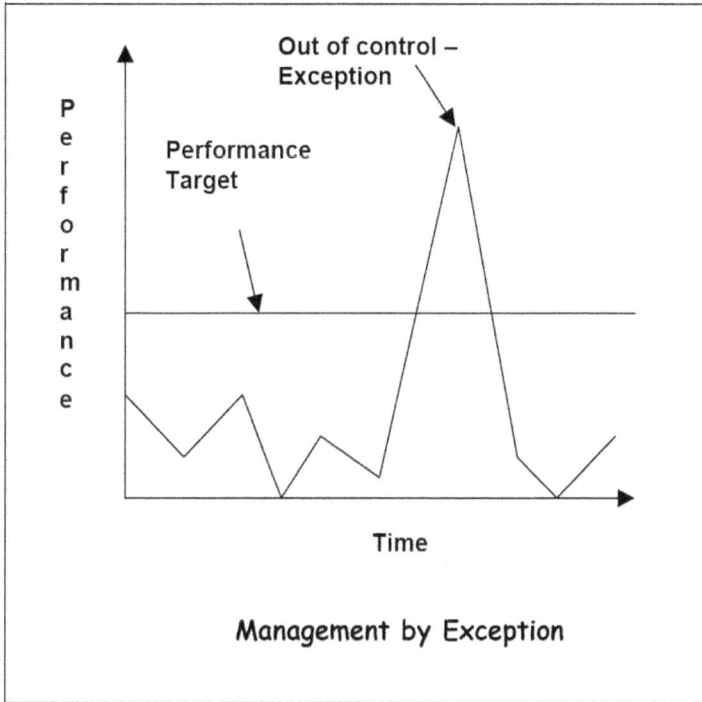

Management by Exception

CUTTING EDGE RISK MANAGEMENT

Supply chain risk management is still in its infancy. A process owner or supply manager may not have measurement systems in place. Without these, supply risk management is difficult. Or, if metrics are available, they may be inaccurate, unreliable, or unrealistic.

The purpose of risk management is to get a better understanding of the supply chain system and key process variables. Process and product risk analysis make it easier to understand the dynamics of what, who, how, when, and where things can go wrong.

In general, the supply manager should be aware of the following regarding risk management:

- Supply chain risks are sometimes unknown and unknowable.

- Supply chain risks interact in unexpected ways.

- Multiple supply variables can have unknown impacts.

- Single variable can interact with others that result in multiple effects.

- Process owners may be too close to the problem.

- Mathematical modeling can provide a false sense of security and accuracy.

RISK MANAGEMENT STRATEGIES

If a supply risk event occurs, recurs, or may occur, the supply manager or process owner has several decision options:

- **Avoid risk.** This requires the root cause of the risk is eliminated. The supply manager may find a more responsive or capable supplier.

- **Mitigate risk.** This requires the probability of the event occurring is reduced. Risks can be mitigated through transferring, deflecting or reducing them. Risks may be mitigated through supply contingency plans, and insurance. Examples of risk mitigation include using redundant suppliers, cross training existing personnel, or using backup hardware.

- **Accept risk.** This means the customer has identified the risk, its consequences, and can live with them. The supply manager accepts the fact that shipments from a supplier may have an acceptable number of nonconforming products. If the quality level of received products needs to be improved then the customer or supplier can invest in additional machinery to improve capability levels.

- **Share risk.** This means the customer and supplier assume and share the risk. The customer may need improved quality from a captive or sole-source supplier and will invest in capital equipment at the supplier's location.

- **Diversify risk.** This means the risk is unacceptable and must be spread out. The supply manager has a sole source supplier and the risk of an event such as a strike implies that shipments may be disrupted. The customer diversifies the risk by finding acceptable alternate suppliers.

- **Control risk.** This means the occurrence or recurrence of the risk can be monitored and even prevented. The supply manager has sufficient trend analysis or other information to predict when a shipment may contain nonconforming products, when a machine's output may be out of specification, or when machines should be preventively maintained.

- **Increase risk.** This means the customer will increase risks because the potential returns outweigh the risks. For example, a company may choose a new supplier to reduce cycle times or increase product development opportunities. The future potential returns outweigh present perceived risks.

MANAGEMENT BY EXCEPTION

A robust supply chain should be stable and capable. In other words, suppliers are relatively high on the capability and maturity curve. This has significant implications to the supply manager. If a process is stable, supply managers can manage the supply chain by exception. If there is an anomaly, discrepancy, nonconformance, constraint, or some other abnormal activity, the supply manager or team can focus their attention on solving the problem. Stable supply processes are the norm. Unstable supply chain events are the exception or the abnormal situation. If there is a system or process spike, it's smarter to have a process that corrects the problem and even anticipates the problem.

CONTEXT: Risk Management Questions

- What risks can the customer accept?
- What risk management strategy does the customer want to follow?
- What role does the process owner want the supply manager to assume?
- What are specific system, process, or product risks?
- What can be done to mitigate each risk variable?
- What approach should be followed, i.e. risk transfer, risk deflection, and risk reduction?
- What happens if risks are accepted?
- What type of contingency plan should be developed?

FOLLOW THE PARETO-PRINCIPLE

The 80-20 rule is the Pareto Principle. The Pareto Principle is a simple example of risk based, decision making. Expressed in supply chain terms, the Pareto Principle says that 20% of the suppliers will cause 80% of the problems. Thus, the Principle identifies the most critical risks to manage. Or expressed another way, the Pareto Principle identifies the most critical supply chain variables that pose the highest risk of failing, not meeting requirements, or causing problems.

SUMMARY

The supply manager should focus his or her time understanding and analyzing critical internal and supply process variables and constraints, specifically those that have a high probability of occurring or can impact quality, time, scope, and cost adversely.

Risk management is simply good supply chain management. A supply manager should prioritize products and services into risk categories. Those with the higher risk and importance are managed more carefully. For example, if the supply manager is dealing with high value, technology, process, or quality content then these are managed more carefully than commodity or price sensitive items.

Supply chain risk management isn't easy. It requires a high level of customer-supply trust. Suppliers may be reluctant to share proprietary cost, margin, and performance information with customers. This makes sense. If a supplier is selling a product at a 30% margin to one customer and only 25% to another, the supplier doesn't want to share this sensitive information for the obvious reason. The customer paying the higher amount will demand the supplier match the lower price.

What does the supply manager do if he or she doesn't have sufficient process knowledge or information to identify risks? The supply manager then must get qualified experts or preferably process owners to identify process risks and controls.

CHAPTER 14: PROCESS AND PRODUCT INNOVATION

Every company is redesigning their internal and supply chain processes to deliver value adding products and services to customers faster. First to market and time to market are competitive differentiators. Product development or time to market, is too long for many companies.

There is usually a wakeup call to transform the product development process. Automakers recognized there was trouble when Japanese automakers were consistently designing and building a new automobile in less than 30 months when the U.S. 'Big Three' automotive manufacturers required 48 to 60 months to accomplish the same set of tasks.[1]

THE NEED FOR NEW PRODUCTS

We're in the age of the idea. The organizations that can develop a culture of creativity and idea generation will be the winners.
Kevin Roberts, CEO, Saatchi & Saatchi

What makes a successful company? Innovative products and stable supply chain processes allow a company to bring products to market quickly and to generate revenue. Steve McConnell, the author of **Rapid Development**, says there are "10 to 1 differences in productivity between companies within the same industries" that develop state-of-the-art processes like SCM.[2]

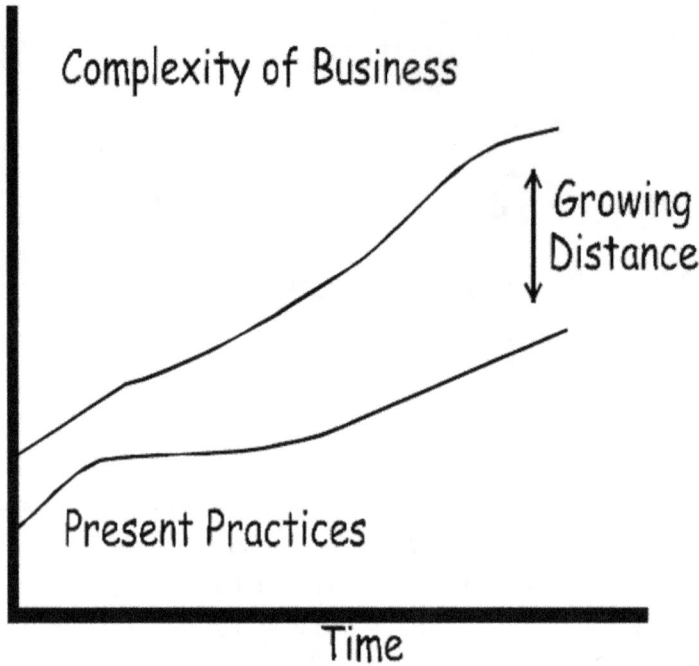

Complexity of Business

Growing Distance

Present Practices

Time

THE COMPLEXITY OF BUSINESS

As business and life become more complex, companies are losing their ability to compete by following their present practices. This delta, the 'growing distance' between the complexity of competitive business practices and the state of present practices, is the zone where supply managers can excel. This zone (see figure on the next page) is where the organizational pain is highest and is where supply managers have the greatest potential to add value.

INNOVATIVE COMPANIES WIN

Fast Company, the innovative business magazine, says to win in business a company has to work smarter not harder. The logic goes like this. If a company wants to win at business, it needs the best people and the best work processes, such as supply chain management.[3]

The *Economist Magazine* made the case for innovative work processes:

> "Innovating has become the buzzword of American manage-
> ment. Firms have found that most of the things that can be out-
> sourced or reengineered have been (worryingly, by their com-
> petitors as well). The stars of American business tend today to
> be innovators, such as Dell, Amazon, and Wal-Mart, which have
> produced ideas or products that have changed their industries."[4]

The financial numbers reinforce the power of innovation. The top 20%
of firms in a *Fortune Magazine* innovation poll had double the shareholder returns of their peers. And, that frightens all companies. It's all
about killer ideas these days – ideas that can change processes, projects, people, organization, organizations, industries, and ultimately society.[5]

PRODUCT DEVELOPMENT MATH

Some companies must develop a new generation of products yearly.
Competition is Darwinian. Although some 13,000 new products hit the
market each year, only 40% will be around 5 years later.[6] The time-to-
market math for new products becomes pretty simple.

Examples of rapid product innovation can be found all over. Hewlett-
Packard wants 80% of its revenues to come from products that are less
than 3 years old. Fashion designs change quarterly. Software is enhanced yearly. Twice as fast computer chips are introduced every eight-
een months. Even in the automotive industry, General Motors wants to
halve product development time from the current minimum 40 months
to 24 months.[7]

MASS CUSTOMIZE OR NOT

Another conventional wisdom in product development seems to have
shifted. Is it true the customer wants freedom of choice in all things?
We're offered many options and features in software and gadgets. The
reality is that we're confused and don't use the additional features. Several examples should illustrate this. At home, I have a control device
for my VCR, TV, stereo, etc. Each device has 10 or 20 control features.
None will talk to each other. I basically use the on/off, volume and

selection changes. That's it. The same can be found with software. I use the most popular office suite and use probably 2 to 5% of its features. What's the benefit of the rest?

Well techno-wizards are getting smarter and have discovered that we don't want the extra bells and whistles or unlimited choice. We want basic value. Not the 'one size fits all' product or service but a good product that can be tailored to satisfy our most needed requirements or in other words a simple mass-customized product. For example, MCI or phone carrier may call you, review your account, discuss your options, look for potential savings, and present one or two choices. Again, the purpose is to offer value and make the product-buy decision simple.[8]

DESIGN CHALLENGE: LISTEN TO THE CUSTOMER

The history of technology is full of neat ideas that didn't work out. Sometimes, the customer had unrealistic expectations. Sometimes, the development team was clueless of what the customer wanted. Sometimes, they didn't connect. These techno-turkeys include all types of products and inventions.[9]

The challenge is to make technology seamless with work or in other words to make technology disappear for the user. People don't need to decipher manuals or write code. The development team needs to think how the supply chain can be integrated to design 'cool', customer-friendly products.

PRODUCT INNOVATION

In the future, more people will work for themselves, creating a huge market for bizarre products.
Scott Adams, 'Dilbert' creator

Supply managers and supply-partners are introduced early into product development.

CONCURRENT PRODUCT DEVELOPMENT

To shrink development cycle times, critical product development activities are often done concurrently instead of sequentially. In concurrent product development, design participants including supply partners can interact in real time, sharing designs, bills of material, and other design images on a computer monitor. The development team uses computers to simulate user requirements, design in 3D, do 'what-if' analyses, and test products under different conditions. Everyone sees the same documents in real time. Documents and drawings are discussed and amended during the meeting. Iterations, redundancies, and costs are eliminated as work is simplified.[10]

While linear product development was time consuming, it offered benefits. The process worked because it was predictable, redundancies ensured that mistakes were caught, and all parties were likely to understand requirements. Concurrent product development can be messy. Communications are more difficult. There are more opportunities for mistakes late in the product life cycle and it's difficult to break the 'toss it over the wall' development mentality.

EARLY SUPPLY INVOLVEMENT

Critical supply chain stakeholders including supply-partners are brought in early in product development. Supply chain involvement in the design process may be as simple as resolving design conflicts such as aligning holes or ensuring parts are accessible for maintenance.

More often, supply managers should be familiar with design technologies, specifically computers and other electronic tools that make cost-effective design possible. Engineers use computers to understand and change designs much like writers use word processors to move words and paragraphs to develop a book.

STORIES OF INNOVATION AND IMPROVEMENT

The following stories of innovation illustrate the importance of supply-partners:

Boeing 777

Product development now utilizes the best people, principles, and practices in virtual teams. Design data is transmitted real time to stakeholders so the virtual team can collaborate on designs. Boeing's engineers and supply-partners designed the 777 jet using a computer-aided-system to develop and assemble a virtual plane so hundreds of thousands of parts fitted perfectly when the first prototype was assembled.

Toyota

Toyota says it can produce a car within 5 days of a custom order. This is startling because the auto industry has often kept customers waiting 30 to 60 days. Why is this important? This is a huge competitive advantage in today's Internet economy, as customers want instant online order gratification. Faced with a long delay, most U.S. customers will settle for what a dealer has on the lot.

How does this work? Toyota auto planners have developed a 'virtual production line.' The system calculates exactly which supplied parts need to be available at each point of the production line so the expected mix of vehicles is determined days prior to actual production.[11]

Swatchmobile

Have you seen Swatches? They are funky, cheap, colorful, and changeable watches. A person can change watches three or more times a day depending on his or her moods, functions to attend, or attire. Swatches for some have evolved in a living and working accessory.

People can now update their automobiles similarly. Daimler-Benz engineers designed a go-cart sized, plastic vehicle called the Swatchmobile to satisfy fickle consumer wants, test-design plastic bodies, and develop supply partnerships. Customers can change the 'look and feel' of their vehicles on a whim and at a nominal cost. The ultra-light, ultra-fuel efficient two seater sells for about $8,500.

Swatchmobile suppliers don't just make handles and headlights. They supply the entire door, front end, or cockpit as modules to be assembled. The suppliers also install the parts so a Daimler supply manager is little more than a product coordinator where most employees are even on someone else's payroll.

Smart Appliances

Talking toasters, smart copiers, and thinking vending machines are coming to the supply chain. Toasters with a chip will recognize simple voice commands like light, dark or burnt toast. When a smart copier or vending machine fails or is about to fail and can't self-correct, it will transmit an email to a technician to come and fix it. Service personnel will fix it just in time as it's about to fail. It will be a stretch for many of us to have a meaningful conversation with our talking toasters or washing machines.[12]

THE ECOMMERCE PROMISE

"The Internet has become a powerful symbol of society's expectation about the future – a future of fast-moving, disruptive technology that is shifting the terrain not only in business, but also in politics and culture.
New York Times*"*[13]

Customer-supply alliances will become common, as more companies understand the benefits of partnering to bring products to market quickly.

USING TECHNOLOGY TO LINK CUSTOMERS AND SUPPLIERS

Technology is creating an interconnected world. Customers, suppliers, engineers, and supply managers can swap technical and market information almost instantaneously with virtual colleagues all around the world.

What's the function of the web in the supply chain? Is the web the backbone of the supply chain or does it facilitate the sourcing process? More often, the Web is seen as the facilitator to accelerate the speed of information flow. At its simplest, the Web frees companies from the cost, time, and errors of clerical transactions.

<hr>

CONTEXT: Types of Innovation

- Me-too products.
- Product improvements.
- Extensions of current lines.
- Novel replacements.
- New-to-the-market products.
- Breakthrough products.[14]

<hr>

Networked companies are critical to concurrent product development. Engineering, quality, manufacturing, customer service, supply management, sales, and suppliers can evaluate and review design information simultaneously. These project teams can view the product on the computer, check calculations, evaluate critical characteristics, conduct tests, evaluate the bills of material, and evaluate the product.

Once a design is developed, special instructions can be downloaded from the computer to production machinery as well as to automatic inspection and testing equipment. What-if and how questions can be answered though the computer often without having to build multiple prototypes.

Supply chains are electronically linking suppliers, customers, distributors, transporters, designers, and other strategic partners. A supply manager can check a supplier's order, delivery dates, invoices, payments, and receipts.

THE MEGA B2B EXCHANGES

A huge sourcing development in the last few years has been the growth of electronic sourcing exchanges. Ford Motor Company is developing the AutoXchange and General Motors is planning the TradeXchange. Ford will purchase more than $77 billion annually while GM will spend about $63 billion through their systems. Each supplier from tier 1 to the end will be electronically linked with the customer. When finished, each supply chain will transact more than $300 billion apiece. Huge by anyone's account.[15]

CONTEXT: Ecommerce Fundamentals

- Automate, automate, and automate.
- Integrate departments within a company that have previously operated as independent silos of information.
- Integrate key supply chain stakeholders so inventory and orders are visible across the chain.
- Collaborate with supply chain partners to fulfill demand at the highest margins.[16]

The exchanges are basically auction sites. Customer requirements and specifications are listed on the site. They are an eBay for industrial products and services. Benefits should accrue to all parties. Buyers can expand their supply base, find better prices, and lower their sourcing costs. Suppliers can better manage their own supply chains, reduce their transaction costs, and reduce their marketing costs.

SUMMARY

A person buys a famous name computer, such as an IBM or a Hewlett Packard and expects it to be made by the company. Guess again. More often no-name manufacturers make computers, printers, cell phones and the high-tech gadgets.

More companies want to focus on their core competencies and outsource other activities. Much of the previous outsourcing trend was low tech and low value added activities to offshore plants. Now, the trend is to outsource more core activities to U.S. contract manufacturing companies. We're seeing virtual companies that do little more than design and market their products while contractors do what they do best.

Supply-partners are also being integrated into the concurrent product development process. This is becoming a core and high-value SCM activity. Supply managers in these organizations know how to measure and integrate supply-partners into concurrent product development.

CHAPTER 15:
SUPPLY CHAIN
MANAGEMENT FUTURE

Even though I'm a great believer in rules, rules assume linearity, stability, and prediction. These are often hard to find in supply chain management. What do I mean? Regardless if you're in supply management, production, engineering, quality, or logistics, the rules change as the game is played. Supply chain rules today are too often chaotic, volatile, or non-linear. Supply chain forecasts are made on wavy assumptions.

SUPPLY CHAIN CHALLENGES

I find the great thing in this world is, not where we stand, as in what direction we are moving.
Oliver Wendell Holmes, Writer

Companies are becoming so efficient that Hewlett Packard, IBM, Texas Instruments and others are handing over more critical manufacturing, quality control, and distribution to suppliers.

VIRTUAL COMPANIES

Companies may evolve into a core group of employees who manage a company's brand and intellectual property. The *Wall Street Journal* warned:

> "The U.S. contract manufacturers are helping hollow out American's corporations while bolstering their manufacturing base.

They (suppliers) land orders because they are considered among the world most efficient manufacturers, and their proximity is prized because it facilitates quick product development."[1]

GHOST CARS – GHOST BRANDS

Forbes Magazine ran a cover story on 'Ghost Cars, Ghost Brands' featuring Bob Lutz, the former Vice Chairman of Chrysler. He is developing an auto company called Cunningham Motor Company that he predicts will have $100 million of annual revenues – all with less than 20 employees. "Cunningham will be the world's most *virtually* integrated car company."[2]

This is the future of supply management. The overarching thread of this book is that companies are going to focus on their core competencies. Cunningham's core competencies are a great business model, unique design, strong management, and great brand. Who will do most of the work at Cunningham? Suppliers. Who will manage the external suppliers? Supply management.

The focus on core competencies and outsourcing noncore work is truly a paradigm shift. Many companies, suppliers, processes, and people are not SCM ready. While companies are outsourcing noncore and even some core activities, the reality is that internal core and supply-partner processes still must be managed.

SEPARATING REALITY FROM HYPE

There is a lot of supply chain hype. For example, business-to-business (B2B) exchanges were supposed to revolutionize the supply chain. Well, the reality is they didn't. Many of the B2B exchanges went out of business. *Wall Street Journal* and *New York Times* articles reported in exact detail why they failed. Usually, new fangled technologies didn't consider the human element including customer-supply relationships, communications, and trust. Far out technology solutions were driven by herd think, over promises, and little understanding of purchasing fundamentals.

CONTEXT: Who Do You Call?

A supply chain program, computer, or ERM/CRM module crashes. Or, built-in product electronics, GPS, or some diagnostic device crashes. This is all too common as buggy software is found in almost all products. Who's going to fix this problem? Who gets the first call? And oh by the way, production has stopped and 500 people are hanging around for that software forecasted, just in time delivery.

That's your wakeup call that supply chain management is tough and technology may not save you. The ERP help desk and customer service at this point seem like oxymorons.[3]

TECHNOLOGY ABILITIES GAP

Customers and suppliers want to move up the process capability and maturity curve. There is only one problem. SCM stakeholders such as supply managers, planners, manufacturing professionals, quality engineers and others can't keep up with technology and the velocity of change. At its simplest, too many purchasing people are still product and transactional focused, not process oriented.

IT'S STILL A PEOPLE BUSINESS

Certain supply management tasks will never be automated because they rely on individual judgment, discretion, and decision-making. For example, supply development, collaboration strategies, 'make or buy' decisions, corrective/preventive actions, and continuous improvement can't be deferred to a software program. Technology may facilitate decision making, but it won't replace people judgment.

EPROCUREMENT CHALLENGES

Eprocurement was supposed to be the answer to all supply chain problems. Well, yes and no. Many pioneering eprocurement projects failed due to technical, political, and cost issues. Let's discuss each. Software vendors over promised and under delivered. The reality was the first supply chain software programs were buggy. IT software vendors frankly didn't understand sourcing issues, which were often company-specific. One-size software didn't fit all companies. Finally, development, application, and tailoring costs spiraled out of sight.

The takeaway for many involved in early ERP, eprocurement and other initiatives is that technology is a tool in a larger context of core process management and the pursuit of profitability.

SCM LESSONS LEARNED

Prediction is very difficult, especially about the future.
Neils Bohr, Nobel Physicist

Supply chain management is an evolving discipline. Patricia Moody, a SCM pundit, wrote:

> "Clearly, the buzz about strategic sourcing and supply chain management is not supported by the data. If the sourcing function controls so much corporate spending - more than 80% in the automotive industry - then why is it still stuck working on short-term problems such as processing paper and tracking orders?"[4]

Why is there a discrepancy between SCM reality and perceptions? The supply management need is well understood, but the people, process, and practices infrastructure aren't there to support the need. There are not enough trained supply managers to fill the demand. Supply chain processes are not mapped or understood. Supply management practices have not kept up with technology.

FIGHTING FLAVOR OF THE MONTH

A critical SCM challenge is the fact that many SCM initiatives may fail within the next few years. Goals aren't reached. Competing but complementary flavors of the month such as just in time management, lean management, or six sigma will compete for management's attention.

SCM is too critical for competitiveness that it should suffer a fad backlash. But, let's look at what happened to Total Quality Management

(TQM). Expectations were built up. TQM was heralded as the panacea, the miracle cure, the way to competitiveness, the holy grail of management, and so on. The problem was that there was a quick fix fixation. Reality set in. Results were less than expected. The silver bullet turned out to be zinc pellet.

SCM may also become faddish. People tend to dismiss instant benefit labels. This happened with MBO, TQM, etc. All of these were useful and offered organizational benefits. Previous technologies promised, perhaps over promised instant pudding benefits and failed. True reform and supply chain transformation take time, require consistent management commitment, and require increased organizational maturity and capability.

THE GOOD NEWS

Supply chain management seems a more holistic and integrated approach to performance improvement than other tools and techniques. We're seeing more senior supply managers, even in executive levels. This is critical because one critical success factor stands out among all others - active senior management support. A journalist reported: "among people with experience, there is consensus on why supply chain management projects succeed or fail: it only works if senior management is committed and involved."[5]

Supply chain management should have a long and prosperous future if developed and deployed properly. The following are my 'lessons learned' from many initiatives that became faddish and eventually failed:

- Lack of senior management commitment.

- Too much exhortation.

- Fear.

- Confusion.

- Special project mentality.

CONTEXT: Why SCM May Not Work

- Requires competitive, enterprise, and process emphasis.
- Requires fundamental cultural, attitudinal and behavioral changes.
- Is not universally understood and appreciated.
- Are no information and ecommerce minimum standards.
- Is knowledge and labor intensive.
- Can develop its own cumbersome bureaucracy.
- Issues such as 'pull,' 'push,' or 'push/pull' demand are not standardized.
- Is driven by information technology buzz and vaporware.
- May require radical organizational and supply chain change.
- Requires new knowledge and skill from people who are still in a transactional, purchasing mode.
- Appeals to faddism.

- Quick fix mentality.

- Far out technology.

- Lack of instant gratification.

Lack of Senior Management Commitment

As mentioned, lack of active senior management commitment and leadership is the major cause of SCM failure. Organizational and supply chain transformation is phenomenally difficult. All supply chain activities must be customer focused and aligned with the organizational vision.

Too Much Exhortation

W. Edwards Deming was right. It's easy to become caught up in the hoopla and excitement of a new initiative, such as SCM. Exhortations, banners, inducements, and publicity are useful at certain stages of the process, but are counter-productive or destructive if used all the time. They lose their effect to induce, promote, or reinforce positive images of supply development and improvement.

When is exhortation useful? Exhortation is useful at the beginning of the process to create SCM value awareness. It is useful at those special occasions when the supply chain celebrates successes. It is also helpful in elevating issues, awareness, and attitudes of the benefits of customer satisfaction, supplier benefits, and continuous improvement throughout the supply chain.

Fear

Fear of change paralyzes people and suppliers. SCM may be slowly adopted by middle purchasing management who can't move from a transaction focus. Suppliers can't or won't adopt the SCM even though the consequence may be elimination from the approved supply bidder's list. Or, internal employees may not adopt lean or six sigma because they are associated with downsizing. Who wants to see his or her job disappear?

Confusion

SCM also may seem difficult because it encompasses a hodgepodge of management principles, techniques, and skills. SCM for many traditional purchasing managers simply doesn't make sense because it integrates benchmarking, inventory management, six sigma, and other new practices.

Special Project Mentality

SCM may seem to the purchasing, functional and operating manager as another special project on top of the daily concerns of moving products out the door on time. A middle manager may have to change the way he or she does a job. This is difficult and is resisted unless a good case can be made to make his or her life easier. Change without a good rationale is always resisted.

Quick Fix Mentality

What manage a supply chain? No problemo. A consulting company may say: "Our enterprise resource planning, customer resource management, or data mining tools will help you do the job." The operative word is 'help' you do the job. The reality is that supply process owners are still responsible for getting the right products and services to the right location on time and on budget. There is no quick fix.

Far Out Technology

Sophisticated technology tools allow a company to model supply processes; mine historical data on nonconformances, late/early deliveries, cost overruns, low product counts; then identify predictive benchmarks which are fed into the model to monitor, control and manage the supply chain. This sounds great on paper but reality bites. There are too many suppliers, processes, people, resources, products, and unknowns that make accurate and reliable forecasting difficult. Most supply chains are nonlinear and often unpredictable.

SUPPLY CHAIN FUTURE

Two roads diverged in a wood, and I –
I took the one less traveled by,
And that has made all the difference.
Robert Frost

Is SCM here to stay? A common criticism is that every two years or so, there is a new killer fad or buzzword. SCM is today's killer performance solution. Management consultants have a tendency to rediscover and repackage concepts that were introduced 10 or even 20 years ago.

CUSTOMER FOCUS

Finally, what makes a great supply chain? It all comes down to final customer satisfaction and having all supply chain stakeholders understand this. Technology, quality management, JIT management and logistics management are only part of the solution. Customer focus and process execution are the key elements of SCM success. The *Economist Magazine* concluded:

> "In the end, durable customer relations are only partly about clever technology, however imaginatively used. Mainly they require relentless attention to detail: good products, prompt service, well-trained staff with the power to do a little extra when

they judge it right to do so. No wonder firms that send you away with a smile on your face are so rare."[6]

KILLER SUPPLY CHAIN TEAMS

The business world where a lone wolf engineer can design a killer product or a transforming leader can save an enterprise single-handed no longer exists. Challenges, problems, and opportunities overwhelm the mightiest, smartest, individual. Great leadership isn't sufficient any longer. Supply management leaders and great teams are needed throughout the chain, at the highest and lowest levels. A major organizational challenge is identifying today's and tomorrow's supply chain leaders.

SEAMLESS ELECTRONIC PROCESSES

At a basic level the Internet is useful for communicating sourcing decisions and for conducting simple transactions. The Internet can be an electronic substitute for paper, phone and fax purchase orders, which provide savings in error elimination, labor reductions, and cost efficiencies. But, this is a far cry from what the business to business (B2B) exchanges promised which was fully integrated beginning-to-end sourcing. This is the technology promise and supply management challenge in the next few years.

The future challenge will be to create seamless, electronic global processes and networks among customers, suppliers, and significant supply chain stakeholders. Huge benefits will accrue to companies that develop these lean and seamless supply processes and networks.

> "Corporate functions once seen as critical - design, production, demand fulfillment, customer care, information creation and management, logistics, procurement (indirect), plus such supply chain management activities as supplier performance measurement - will all be supplied by contractors, making corporations far more 'virtual' than they are today."[7]

SUPPLY MANAGER CAREER DEVELOPMENT

Senior management is well aware that supply management impacts a large number of dollars. Unfortunately, supply management has not matured to become a strategic unit in many organizations.

The corporate desire is to develop world-class, SCM practices but people capabilities are frankly not up to the challenge. For too many years, purchasing agents, buyers, planners and others have learned tactical and tools. The supply paradigm has shifted. The purchasing rules have changed. Tomorrow's supply manager and professional must have more strategic skills.

CORE COMPETENCY ARGUMENT

Supply managers must understand and articulate the core process and outsourcing mantra daily to all stakeholders. Supply managers are the evangelists of this message. They create the daily sense of urgency. This is especially critical because designing a reliable and aesthetically pleasing product is difficult in light of reduced product lifecycles. A 10-year product lifecycle may now be compressed into 2 years or even 1 year. There's little time to adapt or modify the product. Suppliers must be seamlessly integrated to develop and deliver the right products to the customer at the right time. If they're not, the customer will shop around until he or she is satisfied.

THE FUTURE

When a management tool, idea, or philosophy is over promoted, there is a good chance it may become a fad. Organizations try it and lose interest when they don't receive instant gratification.

SCM shouldn't become a fad as long as it continues to add value. All companies must practice some basic level of value chain management, either having minimal consistent processes or having 'world class' processes for companies in highly competitive industries. As well, all companies will have to improve their quality, cost, technology, delivery, and service processes by moving up the capability and maturity curve.

So, "Is SCM here to stay?" I think SCM will flourish as long as supply core processes are aligned and integrated with internal competencies.

INDEX

ENDNOTES

CHAPTER 2: COMPETITIVENESS FUNDAMENTALS

1. Ibid., Vol. 2, p. 6.
2 Kiernan, Matthew, **The Eleven Commandments of 21st Management**, Prentice Hall, 1996, p. 11-13.
[3] Lieber, Ronald, "Why Employees Love These Companies," *Fortune Magazine*, January 12, 1998, p. 74.
1. Robert, Michel, Strategy **Pure and Simple**, New York: McGraw Hill, 1993.
2. "Making Companies Efficient," *Economist*, December 21, 1996, pp. 87-99.
[3] King, Julia, 'Outsourced But Not Outclassed,' *Computerworld Premier 100*, November 16, 1998, p. 36-37.
[4] Dolan, Kerry and Meredith, Robyn, "Ghost Cars. Ghost Brands", *Forbes*, April, 30, 2001, p. 106.
[5] "Anders, David; Britt, Frank, Favre, Donavon, "The Seven Principles of Supply Chain Management, " *Supply Chain Management Review*, Spring 1997.
[6] Cox, James and Blackstone, John, **APICS Dictionary**, APICS, 9th Edition, 1998, p. 93.
[7] Rettig, Hillary, 'Drill Down,' *VARBusiness*, September 9, 1997, p. 139.
[8] "Unleashing Supply Chain Potential," *International Tax Review*, March, 99, p. 28.
[9] Stuart, Ian and McCutcheon, David, Manager's Guide to Supply Chain Management, *Business Horizons*, March/April, 2000, p. 35.
[10] Stuart, Ian and McCutcheon, David, "Manager's Guide to Supply Chain Management," *Business Horizons*, March/April, 2000, p. 35.
11 Barker, Joel, Paradigms: The Business of Discovering the Future, Harper Business, 1992, pp. 32.
[12] Hutchins, Greg, **Working It**, QPE, 2001.
[13] "Experts See Big Future for E-procurement," *Sourcing*, March 23, 2000.
[14] Rose, Robert and Quintanilla, "Sara Lee's Plan to Contract Out Work Underscores Trend Among US Firms," *Wall Street Journal*, March 17, 1997, p. A3.
[15] Biddle, Frederic, "British Airways Moves Closer to Being 'Virtual Airline,' *Wall Street Journal*, June 25, 1998, p. B1.
[16] Wysocki, Bernard, "Defining Challenge: Corporate American Confronts the Meaning of a 'Core' Business," *Wall Street Journal*, November 11, 1999, p. A1.
[17] Brandt, John, "Beyond the Supply Chain," Industry Week, November 2, 1998, p. 6.
18. The four attributes are derived from the definition in B. Enis, **Marketing Principles**, Glenview, IL: Scott, Foresman, 1980, p. 5.
19 Suris, Oscar, "How Ford Cut Costs on Its 1997 Taurus, Little by Little," *Wall Street Journal*, July 18, 1996, B2.
[20] Warner, Fara, "Detroit Says Everything Old is New Again," *Wall Street Journal*, September 3, 1998, p. B1.
[21] Rettig, Hillary, 'Drill Down,' VARBusiness, September 9, 1997, p. 139.
[22] Andrews, Fred, "It's Not the Product That's Different, It's the Process," *NY Times*, December 15, 1999, p. C14.

CHAPTER 4: CUSTOMER FOCUS

1 "Leaders: Keeping the Customer Satisfied," *The Economist Magazine*, July 14, 2001, p. 9.

2 "Got a Good Idea for a New Product," *Wall Street Journal*, May 1, 1997, p. 1.

3.Day, George, **Market Driven Strategy**, NY: The Free Press, 1990, pp. viii-x.

4 "Leaders: Keeping the Customer Satisfied," *The Economist Magazine*, July 14, 2001, p. 64.

5 Maremont, Mark, "New Toothbrush Is Big-Ticket Item," *Wall Street Journal*, October 27, 1998, p. B1.

6 Miller, Scott, "VW Sows Confusion with Common Pattern for Models," *Wall Street Journal*, October 25, 1999. p. A 25.

7 Marsh, Michael, "Buyers Look to Distributors for Supply Chain Services." *Electronic Business*, February, 2000, p. 51.

8.D. Garvin, **Managing Quality**, NY: Free Press, 1988, pp. 49-69.

9.Pearson, Andrall E., "Corporate Redemption and the Seven Deadly Sins," *Harvard Business Review*, May/Jun, 1992, p: 65-75.

10. Johnson, Sharon, "Tour the Software Chamber of Horrors," *Technology Review*, June, 1994, p. 6.

11.Pierson, John, "Ford Labors Over Tiny Buttons and Dials in Quest for a Driver-Friendly Dashboard," *Wall Street Journal*, May, 20, 1996, p. B1.

12.D. Garvin, "What Does Product Quality Really Mean?", *Sloan Management Review*, Fall, 1984, p.32.

13 Deutsch, Claudia, "High Tech Rubber Hits the Road," *NY Times*, July 20, 1996, p. 21-22.

14 McDermott, Christopher; Handfield, Robert, "Concurrent Development and Strategic Sourcing: Do the Rules Change in Breakthrough Innovation?" *Journal of High Technology Management Research*, Spring, 2000.

15 White, Gregory, "Jeep's Challenge: Stay Rugged But Add Room for Golf Clubs," *Wall Street Journal*, August 26, 1998, p. B1.

16 "Leaders: Keeping the Customer Satisfied," *The Economist Magazine*, July 14, 2001, p. 9.

CHAPTER 5: SUPPLY MANAGEMENT STRATEGIES

1."Brown, Tom, "Re-inventing Yourself, *Industry Week*, November 21, 1994, pp. 20-24.

2   Burnell, John, "Change Management the Key to Supply Chain Management Success," *Automatic I.D. News*, April, 99, p. 40.

3 Morgan, James, "CEOs to Sourcing: No time to 'lighten up'," *Sourcing*, February 22, 2001.

4 Schaefer, William, "E-Procurement business Models," NAPM workshop, May 5, 2001.

5 Schaefer, William, "E-Procurement business Models," NAPM workshop, May 5, 2001.

6.Burt Nanus, **Visionary Leadership**, San Francisco: Jossey Bass, 1992, p8

7 13. Morgan, J. "Integrated Supply Chains: How to Make Them Work!" *Sourcing*, May 22, 1997, pp. 32-37.

8.G. Dessler, **Management Fundamentals**, Reston, VA: Reston Publishing Co., 1985, pp. 30-31.

9.Adapted from "Total Quality Management - A Guide for Implementation," *Superintendent of Documents*, DOD 5000.51G, 1989, p. 15.

10.Adapted from "Total Quality Management - A Guide for Implementation," *Superintendent of Documents*, DOD 5000.51G, 1989, p. 15.

CHAPTER 6: SUPPLY CHAIN LEADERSHIP

[1] Scheck, Susan, "CPOs Must Forge Links to CEOs," *Electronic Buyers' News*, November 30, 1998, p. 52.
[2] "Stallkamp to NAPM: Embrace Internet, But Don't Let It Depersonalize Supplier Relationship," Supplier Selection & Management Report, July, 2000.
3. Pennington, Randy G., "The Personal Commitment to Quality," *HR Magazine*, March, 1993, p: 100-101.
[4] Rettig, Hillary, 'Drill Down,' *VARBusiness*, September 9, 1997, p. 139.
5.Hammons, Charles and Maddux, Gary, "The Fine Tuned Organization," *Quality Progress*, February, 1992, pp. 47-48.
[6] . "Paths of Progress," *Industry Week*, December 11, 2000, p. 7.
7 Kiernan, Matthew, **The Eleven Commandments of 21st Management**, Prentice Hall, 1996, p. 122-3.

[8]"The Future of Work: Career Evolution," *The Economist*, January 29, 2000, p. 92.
[9]Handy, Charles, "Corporate Center," *Executive Excellence*, December, 1998.
10 Handy, Charles, Beyond Certainty: The Changing Worlds of Organizations, *Harvard Business School Press*, 1996, pp. 23-33.
[11] Hutchins, Greg, **Working It**, QPE, 2001.
[12]Handy, Charles, "Corporate Center," *Executive Excellence*, December, 1998.
[13] "The Future of Work: Career Evolution," *The Economist*, January 29, 2000, p. 90.
14 D Quinn Mills, **The Rebirth f the Corporation**, John Wiley & Sons, 1991.
15."Management Discovers the Human Side of Automation," *Business Week*, September 29, 1986, p. 71.

CHAPTER 7: SCM TOOLS AND TECHNIQUES

[1]White, Gregory and Warner, Fara, "Bumper Crop: Competition Rises, Car Prices Drop: A New Golden Age?" *Wall Street Journal*, January 9, 1998, p. A1.
[2] Hardy, Quentin and Takahashi, "Motorola Divides Semiconductor Sector in Five Groups to Hasten New Products," *Wall Street Journal*, May 28, 1997, p. B 16.
[3] Jeanmaire, Phillipe, "Lean Manufacturing: Winning the War Against Waste, *Orange County Business Journal*, April 4, 2000, p. 18.
[4] "Leaders: Keeping the Customer Satisfied," *The Economist Magazine*, July 14, 2001, p. 63.
[5] Murphy, Tom; Schreffler, Roger, "*Just in Time Systems*," Ward's Auto World, May 99, p 67.
[6] "A Look at Lean," *Industry Week*, December 12, 1999, p. 88.
[7] Liker, Jeffrey K.; Wu, Yen-Chun, "Japanese Automakers, U.S. Suppliers and Supply-Chain, *Sloan Management Review*, Fall 2000, p. 81.
[8] "Lean Manufacturing Process Needed for Survival," *Fort Worth Business Press*, 09/01/2000, p. 2A.

[9] Lockwood, Diane L.and Modarress, Diane L, "57-61.

[10] Marsh, Jackie, "Lockheed Pioneers 'Lean Manufacturing',' Fort Worth Business Press, June 30, 2000, p. 6.

[11] Liker, Jeffrey K.; Wu, Yen-Chun, "Japanese Automakers, U.S. Suppliers and Supply-Chain, *Sloan Management Review*, Fall 2000.

[12] Liker, Jeffrey K.; Wu, Yen-Chun, "Japanese Automakers, U.S. Suppliers and Supply-Chain, *Sloan Management Review*, Fall 2000, p. 81.

[13] Shand, Dawne, "Six Sigma," *Computerworld*, March 5, 2001, p. 38.

[14] Trent, Robert J and Monczka, Robert M.., "Achieving World-Class Supplier Quality," *Total Quality Management*, Abingdon, August, 1999, pp. 927-938.

[15] Harry, Mikel and Schroeder, Six Sigma: The Breakthrough Management Strategy Revolutionalizing the World's Top Corporations, Doubleday 2000.

16. C. J. McNair and Kathleen H. J. Leibfried, Benchmarking: A Tool for Continuous Improvement.

17.Camp, Robert, Benchmarking: The Search for Industry Best Practices that Lead to Superior Performance, Milwaukee, WI: Quality Press, 1989.

[18] De Toro, Irving, "The Ten Pitfalls of Benchmarking," *Quality Progress*, January, 1995, pp. 61-63.

[19] Rettig, Hillary, 'Drill Down,' *VARBusiness*, September 9, 1997, p. 139.

[20] Cox, James, **APICS Dictionary 9th Edition**, APICS, 1998.

CHAPTER 7: SCM PROCESS MATURITY MODELS

1.Hutchins, Greg, **Sourcing Strategies for Total Quality**, Homewood, IL: Business One Irwin,, 1992, p. 15.

[2] Gibbs, Hope, "Solutions for the Masses," *Export Today's Global Business*, July, 2000, p. 38.

[3] "Lean Manufacturing Process Needed for Survival," *Fort Worth Business Press*, 09/01/2000, p. p2A.

[4] Carbone, James, "For Automotive Purchasers ... The System is the Thing," *Sourcing*, Boston, February 11, 1999, p. 60.

[5] Gould, Lawrence S. "SCM: Another Acronym to Help Broaden Enterprise Management," *Automotive Manufacturing & Production*, March, 98, p. 64.

[6] Trommer, Diane, "Supply Chain Essentials Continue to Elude Executives," *Electronic Buyers' News*, January 1, 1998, p. 70.

[7] Carbone, James, "Buyers Look to Distributors for Supply Chain Services," *Purchasing Magazine*, February 10, 2000, p.50.

[8] Locke, Dick, "Think Demand, Not Supply," *Electronic Buyers' News*, October 10, 1997, p. 60.

CHAPTER 9: SUPPLY DEVELOPMENT PROCESS

[1] Stuart, F. Ian; McCutcheon, David M., "The Manager's Guide to Supply Chain Management," *Business Horizons*, March/April, 2000, p. 35.

[2] "Supply Chain Fundamentals," *Modern Materials Handling*, February, 2001, p. 2.

[3] Stuart, F. Ian; McCutcheon, David M., "The Manager's Guide to Supply Chain Management," *Business Horizons*, March/April, 2000, p. 35.

4 Fitzgerald, Kevin R., "What Buyers Want from Suppliers," *Sourcing*, November 18, 1999, pp. 17-20.

5 Liker, Jeffrey K.; Wu, Yen-Chun, "Japanese Automakers, U.S. Suppliers and Supply-Chain, *Sloan Management Review*, Fall 2000.

6 Labram, Jeremy, "Another Link in the Change," *Director*, March, 2000, p. 80.

CHAPTER 10: SUPPLY DEVELOPMENT CERTIFICATION

1 American National Standard, "Quality Management Systems – Fundamentals and Vocabulary," ANSI/ASQ Q9000 – 2000, p. 5.

2 American National Standard, "Quality Management Systems – Fundamentals and Vocabulary," ANSI/ASQ Q9000 – 2000, p. 6.

3.Hutchins, Greg, **ISO 9000**, Vermont: Essex Junction, OMNEO, 1993, pp. 145-177.

CHAPTER 11: SUPPLY DEVELOPMENT – CONTINUOUS IMPROVEMENT

1 American National Standard, "Quality Management Systems – Fundamentals and Vocabulary," ANSI/ASQ Q9000 – 2000, p. 11.

2. ISO 9001:2015, ISO Quality Management System, 2015.

3 ISO 9001:2015, ISO Quality Management System, 2015.

4 Trebilcock, Bob, "Welcome to E-world," Manufacturing Systems, *Supply Chain Yearbook*, Wheaton 2000, pp. 87-98.

5 Stuart, F. Ian; McCutcheon, David M., "The Manager's Guide to Supply Chain Management," *Business Horizons*, March/April, 2000, p. 35.

6.This chapter was excepted from Hutchins, Greg, **Sourcing Strategies for Total Quality**, NY: Dow Jones Irwin, 1992.

CHAPTER 12: SUPPLY DEVELOPMENT - MEASUREMENT

1 Klobus, Kenneth, "Measuring Supplier Performance," *Business Journal*, June 4, 1999, p. 2.

2 Stundza, Tom, "Boeing Careful When Picking 'The Best'", *Sourcing*, November 16, 2000, p. 106-107.

CHAPTER 13: INTRODUCTION TO SUPPLY RISK MANAGEMENT

3 Allen, Michael, "Another Jack Welch Isn't Good Enough," *Wall Street Journal*, November 22, 1999, p. A22.

4 Ewing, Terzah, "Carbide CEO to Forfeit Pay if Goal is Missed," *Wall Street Journal*, September 25, 1997, p. A3.

5 "Work Week," *Wall Street Journal*, April 6, 1999, p. A1.

6 Collins, James and Porras, Jerry, **Built to Last**, NY: Random House, 1994.

7 Stundza, Tom and Milligan, Brian, "How Chrysler Will Cut Costs," *Sourcing* Boston, February 8, 2001, pp. 30-32.

1 Chimerine, Lawrence, "The New Economic Realities in Business," *Management Review*, January, 1997, p. 13.

[2] IA, "Standards for the Professional Practice of Internal Auditing," Glossary, November 14, 2000.

[3] IIA, "Standards for the Professional Practice of Internal Auditing," Glossary, November 14, 2000.

[4] COSO, "Key Concepts: COSO Definition of Internal Control," *COSO Home Page*.

[5] COSO, "Key Concepts: COSO Definition of Internal Control," *COSO Home Page*.

CHAPTER 14: PROCESS AND PRODUCT INNOVATION

[1] Gaynor, "Concurrent Development And Strategic Outsourcing: Do The Rules Change In Breakthrough Innovation?," *Journal of High Technology Management Research*, Spring, 2000.

[2] McConnell, Steve, **Rapid Development**, Microsoft Press, 1996, p. xiii.

[3] "New Rules of Business," *Fast Company*, The Greatest Hits, Volume 1, p. i.

[4] "Fear of the Unknown," *The Economist*, December 4, 1999, p. 61.

[5] "Fear of the Unknown," *The Economist*, December 4, 1999, p. 61.

[6] Gustke, Constance, "Built To Last," *Sales & Marketing Management*, August, 1997, pp.78-83.

7 Blemenstein, Rebecca, "GM is Seeking to Speed Up Development," *Wall Street Journal*, August 9, 1996, p. A3.

[8] Pine, Joe, "Customer's Don't Want Choice, *Wall Street Journal*, April 18, 1998, p. A12.

[9] Edson, Lee, "Bold and Costly Blunders," *Across the Board*, June, 1998, pp. 43-48.

10. Suris, Oscar, "Behind the Wheel," *Wall Street Journal*, November 18, 1996, p. R14.

[11] Simison, Robert, "Toyota Develops a Way to Make a Care Within Five Days of a Custom Order," *Wall Street Journal*, August 6, 1999, p. A4.

[12] Weber, Thomas, "Talking Toasters: Companies Gear Up For Internet Boom In Things That Think," *Wall Street Journal*, August 27, 1998, p. A1.

[13] Lohr, Steve, "The Economy Transformed, Bit by Bit," *NY Times*, December 20, 1999, p. C1.

[14] Gaynor, G.H., **Exploiting Cycle time in Technology Management**, New York: McGraw Hill, 1993.

[15] Ford and GM Drive to Build E-procurement Systems," *Sourcing*, February 10, 2000, 139-140.

[16] Trebilcock, Bob, "Welcome to E-world," *Manufacturing Systems, Supply Chain Yearbook*, Wheaton 2000, pp. 87-98.

[1] Thurm, Scott, "Solectron Becomes a Force in 'Stealth Manufacturing," *Wall Street Journal*, August 18, 1998, p. B4.

CHAPTER 15: THE SUPPLY CHAIN MANAGEMENT FUTURE

[2] Dolan, Kerry and Meredith, Robyn, "Ghost Cars. Ghost Brands.' *Forbes*, April, 30, 2001, p. 106.

[3] Deutsch, Claudia, "Succor for Sickly Contraptions," *NY Times*, June 21, 1998, p. 12.

[4] Moody, Patricia, "Strategic Sourcing Remains an Oxymoron," *Sloan Management Review*, Winter 2001, p. 18.

[5] Burnell, John, "Change Management the Key to Supply Chain Management Success," *Automatic I.D. News*, April, 99, p. 40.

[6] "Leaders: Keeping the Customer Satisfied," *The Economist Magazine*, July 14, 2001, p. 10.

[7] "Purchasing 2010," *Purchasing Magazine*, December 22, 2000, p. S6.

www.ingramcontent.com/pod-product-compliance
Lightning Source LLC
Chambersburg PA
CBHW081057220326
41598CB00038B/7130